Secrets of

DIGITAL QUILTING—
FROM CAMERA TO QUILT

✧ 8 PROJECTS ✧ 25 TECHNIQUES ✧ EMBELLISH WITH PAINTS, INKS & MORE

Lura Schwarz Smith and Kerby C. Smith

C&T PUBLISHING

Publisher: Amy Marson

Creative Director: Gailen Runge

Acquisitions Editor: Susanne Woods

Editor: Lynn Koolish

Technical Editor: Wendy Mathson

Copyeditor/Proofreader: Wordfirm Inc.

Cover Designer: Kristen Yenche

Book Designer: Kerry Graham

Production Coordinator: Casey Dukes

Production Editor: Julia Cianci

Photography: Student quilts photographed by Christina Carty-Francis and Diane Pedersen of C&T Publishing, Inc. All other photography by Kerby C. Smith, unless otherwise noted.

Published by C&T Publishing, Inc., P.O. Box 1456, Lafayette, CA 94549

Library of Congress Cataloging-in-Publication Data

Smith, Lura Schwarz.

Secrets of digital quilting—from camera to quilt : 8 projects, 25 techniques : embellish with paints, inks & more / Lura Schwarz Smith and Kerby C. Smith.

   p. cm.

 Includes index.

 ISBN 978-1-57120-659-6 (soft cover)

 1. Textile painting. 2. Textile printing. 3. Quilting. I. Smith, Kerby C. (Kerby Chambless), 1948- II. Title.

 TT851.S63 2010

 746.6--dc22

                    2009020107

 Printed in China

 10 9 8 7 6 5 4 3 2 1

CONTENTS

DEDICATION

To the boundless, irresistible creative spirit within us all that inspires us to produce art.

ACKNOWLEDGMENTS

To our students, enormous thanks for all they teach us and their willingness to bravely step out of their own comfort zones to explore new creative paths.

Special thanks to Lynn Koolish and the C&T crew for all the great help and inspiration. We couldn't have done it without you!

Among our many blessings, we recognize those who appreciate and encourage our art— even the casual passerby who takes a moment to enjoy one of our works and say a kind word.

And thanks forever to our families, who have always supported us, even when the classic mom-and-dad duties may have suffered. One must have one's priorities, and they never failed to believe in the pursuit of art as more important than cooking and laundry—which, by the way, is more often than not done by Kerby.

There are many mentors in our lives, and one of them has been Fresno's Man of Steel, sculptor Chris Sorensen. He proves that art is part of life, liberty, and the pursuit of happiness.

INTRODUCTION

Some years back, when Kerby began to print his images on photographic canvas to show in galleries, Lura realized, "Hey, that's a kind of *fabric*! Let's print some on quilt-weight fabric so they can be cut up and used in a quilt." And so we began to explore the great fun of printing digital imagery on fabric to use in quilting.

Successful printing on fabric is different from printing on paper or photo canvas. It took time and testing to achieve the vivid color and results we wanted. Kerby, with his technical background and close-up knowledge of a quilter's needs, has demystified the process to make it accessible to all.

We live in a world where technology enables us to do things we never could do before, such as printing our own digital fabric at home. But if the "how" gets in the way of the doing, it is frustrating to no end. In this book we give you the power of the digital world in an easy-to-use system. We share with you our system for editing pictures, printing them on fabric, and using that fabric to create a quilt.

Technology will continue to evolve, with new cameras, printers, and software. But the artistic process doesn't change: you still see and take a picture and then edit the image and print it on fabric using your home computer.

In answer to the constantly changing technology, we also provide you with access to our website, www.thedigitalquilt.com, where we discuss the computer hardware and software that we use to make our fabric. Visit the Secrets page of our website for updates to the computer screenshots in this book.

The more we all learn, the richer our toolboxes of options become. Together we can explore new possibilities, tools, and techniques. And best of all, on our continuing art journey, we can approach each new project as an opportunity to try new things, challenge ourselves, and continue to learn and grow.

HOW TO USE THIS BOOK

The projects included in this book demonstrate some of the many techniques you can use when you print your own digital fabrics. These projects, which are meant to inspire, are not geared for exact duplication. Instead, they provide examples of how to explore the various techniques. The projects explain what worked for us, and we hope they will inspire you to explore further on your own.

Even if you don't plan to make the projects, reading through them and trying the techniques will give you tools and tips that can be applied to your own work. We offer these key elements:

- Tips on the best use of your camera and computer software for successful digital printing on fabric

- Lessons on how to enhance your printed fabric with surface design materials

- Information on how to apply the basic elements of design to your work

- Projects that demonstrate how we applied these elements to art quilts

Everyone has her or his own ideas, interests, and images. It's much more meaningful to produce original pieces of art from your own unique images. Study our techniques and projects to add new elements to your existing toolbox. Even if you've never used photo-editing software before or printed your own images on fabric, all you need is an adventurous spirit. Most of all, have fun!

NOTE: If you are new to quiltmaking, refer to Resources (page 94) for our recommendations on several basic quiltmaking books. The project instructions in this book assume basic quiltmaking knowledge.

what you need to print on fabric

Sikiel, Angel of the Sirocco, 48" × 36",
by Lura Schwarz Smith, 2006.

As you read through this book, keep your
vision and needs in mind—in the end, you,
as the creative person, know what you want
your fabric, and ultimately your quilt, to look
like. For example, does the vision for your
quilt come from the tradition of recycling old
fabrics—or in this case, old images—that you
want to print on fabric? Or does your vision
require bold new images printed on fabric?

BEFORE YOU START:
BE AWARE OF COPYRIGHTS

Obviously, as an artist, the best images to use in your
art are your own. They express your own individual
creativity better than anything else. And using your
own unique images to print on fabric for an art quilt
is the best guarantee that you own the copyright to
them and the quilt.

Just as you own the copyright to your original images,
other people own the copyright to the images or
pictures they take. Naturally, the right thing to do
when using something that belongs to someone else
is to ask his or her permission. Remember, if you
copy, scan, or download someone's picture, that
person is the copyright holder to the original image.

Glass House, 39" × 32",
by Lura Schwarz Smith, 2007.

Kerby took this photo of John Lennon and Yoko
Ono in 1973 and owns the copyright for the image.

▶▶ continued on page 6

EQUIPMENT

Here is the basic setup: you need a computer, an inkjet printer, and a way to get pictures into your computer. If you own a home computer and have an inkjet printer, you already have at least two of the things you need to print on fabric.

Computers

The kind of computer you use is up to you. It can be a PC or a Mac, or if you are a real techie, it can be an exotic UNIX machine, as long as it runs photo-editing software. The purposes of the computer are to run a photo-editing program, provide storage for your images, and send the final version of those images to the printer.

Once you have a digital file of your image, whether from a scanner or a digital camera, you need photo-editing software to manipulate that image for the best printout.

Although there are a variety of programs, we focus on the inexpensive program from Adobe, Photoshop Elements, which at the time of this writing is version 7.0. This program is available for both PCs and Macs.

Photoshop Elements is a very powerful stand-alone program. The basic difference between it and the Creative Suite version of Photoshop is that Elements is designed for use with home inkjet printers. The nice thing about Photoshop Elements is that even though each version is a stand-alone program, anything you learn in it applies to its next release, as well as to Photoshop Creative Suite, a program that adds functions for commercial printing.

New models of computers, printers, software, and cameras come out regularly—every two years (or less), there are better, faster, cheaper computers on the market. In addition to faster computers, software gets updated as well. However, the principles behind the system we teach for getting your images on fabric are the same. There are just more choices in hardware and material to get it done. One thing we would like to emphasize is, **start with the equipment you have now**.

Scanners

There are two basic ways to get your images into the computer so you can print them on fabric: scanners and digital cameras.

Some of the many things you can scan are old family photos, drawings, and other artwork. You can scan leaves, flowers, your own hand, keys, and jewelry—just about anything you can put on the scanner glass. The one thing to keep in mind is that scanning is very flat—there is not much depth to the images you get from scanning items placed on the scanner.

If you have an all-in-one inkjet printer that allows you to make copies, then you have a scanner built into it. There are also dedicated scanners. The most common is the flatbed scanner. Some flatbed scanners come with accessories that allow you to scan film negatives and transparencies. However, if you want the best quality scan from your old slides, a dedicated film and transparency scanner is the best way to go.

All of the scanners come with their own software that quickly and easily turns your scanned images into digital files that can be processed by your computer.

Digital Cameras

Digital cameras are everywhere. They come in all sizes, shapes, and prices. You can even find them in cell phones. Many video cameras include a single-shot camera mode. There are simple point-and-shoot digital cameras and digital single-lens reflex (DSLR) cameras that look like older 35mm film cameras. In fact, many of the new DSLR cameras can use the interchangeable lenses from your old 35mm camera system.

Digital photos are measured in pixels. The word *pixel* is a contraction of **pict**ure **el**ement. The sensitivity of the photosensor (the chip inside the camera that records the image) in digital cameras is described by the number of pixels on it. The number of pixels on a photosensor is usually referred to in millions. A million pixels is a megapixel. Digital cameras are referred to as having 3, 6, 10, 12, 21, 39, or more megapixels (MP). Generally speaking, to get a good crisp image with good color on an 8½″ × 11″ piece of paper or fabric, you need to start with a digital image that was taken with at least a 6 megapixel camera.

As of this writing, if you are looking to purchase a digital camera to print your pictures on fabric, you'll want a camera with a minimum of 10–12 megapixels. You can buy both simple point-and-shoot and DSLR cameras with that sensitivity.

▶▶ *Secret*
MEGAPIXELS ARE KING

The more megapixels in your original digital image, the better the image will be when it is printed.

Photo-Editing Software

Once you have a digital file of your image, whether it is from a scanner or a digital camera, you need photo-editing software so you can manipulate the image for the best printout. Although a variety of programs are available, we focus on Photoshop Elements (version 7.0), the inexpensive program from Adobe. Photoshop Elements is available for both PCs and Macs.

▶▶ *Secret*
TRY IT FOR FREE

If you are wondering if Photoshop Elements is for you, Adobe usually offers a free trial version that you can download from their website at www.adobe.com.

Printers

There are two basic types of inkjet printers: those that use dye-based inks and those that use pigmented ink. While you might think that dye-based inks are more durable because they change the color of the fibers, the dyes used in inkjet printers must conform to very strict toxicity and emission controls. In our experience, when used to print on fabric, these dyes are not necessarily durable. They can fade in as little as six months, and even after being chemically set, they can wash out if you are making a quilt that is intended to be washed.

Pigmented inks contain binding agents that help the solid pigment particles adhere to the surface of the fabric and that prevent them from being removed by casual abrasion. The pigments are more lightfast than the dyes, and through advanced aging tests, they have in many cases been labeled archival.

PRINTER RESOLUTION

Inkjet printers spray microscopic dots of ink onto paper and fabric. The resolution of those dots is similar to the pixels in your image. In digital terms, it is referred to as pixels per inch (ppi); in printer terminology, it is referred to as dots per inch (dpi). Each printer manufacturer has an optimum setting for the number of dots per inch for its printer(s).

In general, Hewlett-Packard inkjet printers print at a multiple of 300 dpi. With Hewlett-Packard printers, you get the best results if your image is at 300 ppi. Epson printers work best with images that are a multiple of 360 dpi and are capable of spraying dots as small as 28,800 dpi. For printing with Epson printers, you get the best results if you save your images at 360 ppi.

What happens if you don't match your image to your printer? The printer has to interpolate (add or subtract) the difference between the pixels in your image and what it can output. If you are printing on an Epson printer with a native resolution of 360 ppi and your digital image file has a resolution of 300 ppi, then the printer has to interpolate the difference in pixels. The result is a print that is not as sharp. Check the manufacturer's specifications or printer manual to see what it is optimized for—that is, whether it is a multiple of 300 or 360 dots per inch.

▶▶ Secret

For the best printing results, match your image in pixels per inch (ppi) to your printer's output in dots per inch (dpi).

PRINTING ON FABRIC SHEETS

Fabric needs to be attached or laminated to a backing sheet to stabilize it for printing with inkjet printers. Cotton poplin is the most common laminated fabric sheet for quilting. Although you could laminate fabric to freezer paper and run it through your printer, this does not give the best results in terms of great color on fabric.

Almost all the commercially available paper-backed fabric sheets have a coating on them to attract the ink. The chemicals on top of the fabric are ink receptors. Most of the companies making these sheets have scientists who create their secret formula coatings to give you the best color on their fabric sheets.

If you do try laminating fabric to freezer paper with an iron, there is a high likelihood that the fabric will separate from the backing paper and jam your printer. To make it easier to get home-laminated fabric to run through your printer, tape the leading edge of the fabric to the freezer paper.

At right are examples of different commercial fabric sheets, all printed with the same image through an Epson printer with pigmented inks (in this case, Epson Ultrachrome K3 inks).

Jenkins Miracle Fabric Sheets

Color Plus Fabrics Cotton Poplin Fabric Sheets

EQ Printables Cotton Satin Fabric Sheets

WASHING DIGITAL FABRIC

Inkjet-printed fabric is best used in art and wall quilts that won't be washed. If you are making a quilt or item that will be laundered, you can reduce fading by washing it in cold water with a quilt-wash product such as Orvus Paste or QuiltWash, by soaking it in the delicate or hand wash cycle on your washing machine, or by handwashing. Do not put other clothes in the washer, as they might abrade the fabric.

If you are using a dye-based ink printer, you will get better results if you set the inks with a product like Bubble Jet Set or a concentration of a fabric softener such as Downy.

For pigmented inks, you do not need to set the fabrics before you wash them.

The only downsides to inkjet printers that use pigmented inks are that they are more expensive to buy and the replacement cartridges are more expensive than dye-based ink cartridges. The classic axiom applies here—you get what you pay for; so if you want better color on your fabric that will last longer, use inkjet printers with pigmented inks.

Color Plus Fabrics Cotton Poplin printed on an HP printer with dye-based inks, before washing

Color Plus Fabrics Cotton Poplin printed on an Epson printer with pigmented inks, before washing

Color Plus Fabrics Cotton Poplin printed on an HP printer with dye-based inks, chemically set with Downy fabric softener, after washing

Color Plus Fabrics Cotton Poplin printed on an Epson printer with pigmented inks, after washing

KEEP IT SIMPLE!

If you are just starting to print your own images on fabric, start with what you have, and play with the different techniques to find out the best way to express your creativity. You can always buy better cameras, better computers, and better inkjet printers later on.

> ▶▶ Secret
>
> The creative vision comes from you—
> the equipment just makes it happen.

Glass House, 39" × 32", by Lura Schwarz Smith, 2007.

Get Great Images and Color on Fabric

Angel of Roses, 32″ × 35″, by Lura Schwarz Smith, 2009.

Earlier we talked about your creative vision as a quilt artist and how you can best translate that vision to fabric. Your goal is to create a quilt. If you let the technology get in the way, you risk losing your original vision.

Taking pictures is more important than what they are taken with, as seen in Lura's quilt *Shadowplay* (page 84). She used a simple point-and-shoot digital camera to take the photographs of the chairs and their shadows at the Getty Museum in Los Angeles, California.

This digital photo, which was taken by Lura with an older point-and-shoot camera, is the central image in her quilt *Shadowplay* (page 84).

The image of the "Angel" was drawn by Lura and then scanned on a flatbed Epson scanner to create a digital file. The scan file was a TIFF, and it was imported into Adobe Photoshop Elements to create a Master file. A target or print file was used to generate the fabric printed on Color Plus Cotton Poplin. Kerby's rose images were printed on silk chiffon and silk charmeuse fabric, also from Color Plus. All of the images, whether scanned or original digital photographs, were printed using an Epson printer with Ultrachrome K3 inks. The "Angel's" hands were drawn and inked directly onto fabric by Lura.

DO YOU NEED A NEW CAMERA?

You need to be aware of the camera bug; it is almost as contagious as the flu bug. Someone infected with it runs at the mouth, talking about Canon, Hasselblad, Leica, Panasonic, Sony, Nikon, megapixels, point-and-shoot, digital single-lens reflex, color space, zoom lenses, and so on.

Our philosophy is to use the camera you have and maximize its settings to get the best results. When that camera no longer produces images that convey your vision as an artist, then it is time to get a different camera.

GETTING THE MOST FROM YOUR CAMERA

Whether you have a 3 MP point-and-shoot camera or a 22 MP DSLR, use all the pixels you have. Avoid the temptation to use a lower camera resolution so you can fit more pictures on one memory card. Lura's 6 MP point-and-shoot camera was set at the highest resolution and the largest file size for the pictures she took at the Getty Museum. She used all the pixels she had available to her.

Even if the images look great on your computer screen, you'll be disappointed when you print them on paper or on fabric. Here's why: Most computer screens have a resolution of just 72 pixels per inch, so they don't need a lot of pixels in the image to look good on screen. But if you are printing an image on paper or on fabric, inkjet printers can print up to 28,800 dots per inch. When you have a small picture file, you don't have the pixels to produce a good picture on an 8½″ × 11″ sheet.

IF YOU WANT A NEW CAMERA, WHAT IS BEST?

Digital cameras come in all sizes and price ranges, and the technology is constantly changing. You have to be a dedicated camera nut just to keep up with what is new. Even professional photographers have a difficult time affording the greatest and newest technology.

It is better to have a compact point-and-shoot camera with you when you see that great picture than to have no camera at all. An expensive DSLR camera that is big and heavy is no good if you leave it at home.

Kerby's professional camera bag weighs almost 20 pounds, whereas Lura's compact point-and-shoot camera weighs less than 6 ounces.

There was a point in my life when I was doing more writing than photography. When I traveled, I did not want to haul along my big, heavy camera bag with the professional DSLR camera and all the lenses. But being a die-hard photographer, I had to have a camera with me; so I stuck a small digital point-and-shoot camera in my briefcase.

It was spring and the skies were heavy with rain as we drove across California's central coast. Passing a vineyard, someone had painted the irrigation pipes and shed a brilliant green that absolutely glowed under the overcast skies. I stopped for a few minutes and recorded the scene. I vowed someday to come back with a "real" camera to photograph it properly.

It was a couple of years before I went that way again, but remembering the brilliant green shed, I carried along my "real" camera and all of its lenses. When I reached the vineyard, I was aghast. Someone had repainted that shed a dull mud brown, and the magic was gone.

Green farm shed photo that Kerby took with a point-and-shoot digital camera, thinking he would later go back and shoot with a "real" camera.

The key to finding the right camera is knowing enough about the camera technology so that you are not frustrated. You are the image maker; the camera is just a recorder. What you want is to have your images reproduced on fabric the way you see them.

DIGITAL SINGLE LENS REFLEX VS. POINT-AND-SHOOT

Do DSLR cameras give you better results, even though many of them use the same photosensors that are used in compact point-and-shoot cameras? The answer is yes, because the DSLR cameras have better glass in front of the photosensor. In other words, the optics of modern interchangeable lenses is far superior to what is available in small compact cameras.

One of the most annoying things about compact point-and-shoot cameras is the lag between pressing the shutter release and the click of the picture being taken. The reason for this delay is that the chip that is the camera's photosensor also doubles as the chip that does the automatic focusing. Having one chip do both things keeps the cost down and the size of the camera small.

Larger DSLR cameras have two chips—one for focusing and one for recording the picture—which is why this type of camera can take the picture almost instantaneously when you press the shutter release. One of the biggest advantages of the new generation of full-frame sensors in DSLR cameras is that the photosensor is larger and can hold more pixels.

Camera File Formats

The other major advantage that DSLR cameras have over point-and-shoot cameras is that they offer better software and more options on file format. Many point-and-shoot cameras only allow you to shoot pictures in the JPEG file format. Some let you shoot in TIFF format. But only the top-of-the-line compact cameras let you shoot in RAW. An interesting twist in the camera market is that you can now buy entry-level DSLR cameras for less than the more expensive point-and-shoot cameras.

FILE TYPES

RAW files store the highest level of detail, without any interpretation or restructuring, and are the largest file available on DSLRs and high-end point-and-shoot cameras.

TIFF files store data in an uncompressed format and are relatively large. Store your images as TIFFs as you work on them.

JPEG files store data in a compressed format. Every time you resave a file in JPEG format, it gets compressed again and a little more detail is lost. JPEGs are the smallest files. If you need a small file size, save your image as a JPEG after you have done all the manipulation or processing that you plan to do.

▶▶ Secret

> If you can, take pictures using the RAW file format to get the most flexibility in processing your images.

The JPEG file format is a universal format that compresses the information in the file so it does not take up as much storage on your memory card. Uncompressed file formats, such as TIFF and RAW, are larger files and use more storage space. Again, any time you save space, you lose quality. Generally speaking, you will need a DSLR camera if you want to record your images in an uncompressed file format.

There are also huge advantages to shooting in the camera's RAW format. This format uses all of the information gathered by the photosensor without any restructuring or interpretation by the camera's software. Working with a RAW format file gives you the most flexibility in processing the image your camera recorded.

The only downside with using the RAW format is that you must have software that allows you to process that file. This leads us to another reason that we believe Adobe Photoshop Elements is such a great editing program and a bargain: it comes with a RAW processor as part of the software package. Most digital cameras that allow you to record a RAW file will also let you shoot a JPEG at the same time. This is especially helpful if you are not yet comfortable with processing the RAW files.

Camera Color Space

Color space is the range of color that can be recorded, displayed on-screen, and printed out.

The two common color spaces are sRGB and AdobeRGB. Point-and-shoot cameras only use the sRGB color space, which is more limited; DSLR cameras give you the option of using the larger color range of AdobeRGB.

The menu for color space on most DSLR cameras is often hard to find. However, it is worth the look. If you are printing on an inkjet printer and you have a DSLR, then you want the option of the extended color space offered by AdobeRGB.

On most DSLR cameras, if the camera is set to the Auto mode, the color space menu will be grayed out, meaning it is not accessible. This means you'll be shooting in the sRGB mode. Take your camera off Auto, and set it to the Aperture Priority mode, for example; suddenly the menu for color space will be active, and you can change to AdobeRGB.

▶▶ Secret

> If you are printing on an inkjet printer, switch your DSLR camera's color space to AdobeRGB to get more color in your prints.

GREAT COLOR FOR QUILTERS

The major complaint most people have when substituting fabric sheets through their inkjet printer in place of regular or even photo-quality paper is that the color is dull on the fabric—or, even worse, there was a color shift.

Some people think they can soft proof their pictures on-screen, meaning they think they can tell how their pictures will print out just by looking at them on the screen. Only if you have a true understanding of color management theory and a huge amount of computer savvy will you be able to come close to getting an image on your computer screen that will look similar to the print coming out of your inkjet printer.

The reality is that the image on the computer screen is created by projected light and that the image on a piece of paper or fabric is seen by reflected light. When seen under the right light source, high-quality inkjet papers (often labeled photo paper) with a semigloss or gloss finish can give the impression of the depth that you see when looking at the projected image on a computer screen.

Normally, it is even more difficult to make the comparison between what you see on the screen and what you see on the printed image when you look at a piece of printed cloth. Light simply reflects differently off a piece of cotton poplin than it does off a piece of glossy photo paper. And neither can compare to the brilliance of looking at the same color image on a backlit computer screen.

In the end, the goal is to produce the best color you can on fabric, realizing that the color you see on your computer screen is just a guide. This also means that you will have to adjust the pictures you take so they look their best when printed on fabric.

The simple process we use is to create a Master file with all the adjustments in it for the best image. From that Master file you will then create many outputs, or Target files, that you can adjust based on how you will use them, such as printing on paper, printing on fabric, or sending out as e-mail (see The Digital Quilt System on pages 17–19.)

How We See Color

Before we go into the Master file process, you need to understand the basics of how we see color.

Let's start with one of our favorite subjects—roses. If you look at a red rose at high noon in bright sunshine, it looks different from how it looks when sitting in the shade late in the day. But does the rose really change colors?

If we consider daylight to be the standard for judging color, then the color of a red rose in the shade will have more of a blue-green cast to it. At the other end of the color temperature scale, the same red rose under incandescent light will be more yellow-red.

Photographed in bright daylight

Photographed in afternoon shade—note that the light in the shade is bluer.

Photographed in the evening under a household incandescent light—note that the incandescent light is much yellower than the daylight.

White Balance for the Right Color

Digital cameras use a White Balance setting to get the color right. The most commonly used setting is Automatic White Balance, which adjusts the color to the light. Some Auto settings work better than others, which is why it is important to know about the color of light.

If you take a picture in the shade on the Auto setting and the color is not right, you may need to manually adjust to the Shade setting. Other settings include Daylight, Flash, and Incandescent, among others. Take some time to look at your camera's manual and try out the different settings for White Balance.

Don't panic if you don't get the White Balance setting right. Photoshop Elements offers several ways to adjust the color temperature. There are also specific adjustments you can make to get great images on fabric (see pages 26–27).

COLOR TEMPERATURE

The color we see every day in the world around us varies according to the light's color temperature. In bright sunlight, the color temperature of sunlight varies from 5200 to 5500 degrees Kelvin (K). Shade ranges from 7500 K to 8000 K. At the other end of the color scale is candlelight, at 1850 K, and regular incandescent bulbs, at 3000 K. The colors of fluorescent lightbulbs vary greatly. Warm white bulbs have a color temperature of 3000 K, cool white bulbs are 4100 K, and daylight fluorescent bulbs are 6500 K.

Some cameras allow you to adjust the White Balance to a specific color temperature.

process your pictures for printing on fabric

My Little School in the Redwoods, 41″ × 33″, by Sally A. Swanson, 2008. Quilted by Home Lovin' Quilting.

THE DIGITAL QUILT SYSTEM: GETTING YOUR ORIGINAL IMAGES READY TO PRINT

Processing digital photographs can be as easy or complex as you want to make it. If you like, you can take the editing and manipulation of images to levels you never before imagined possible—all without a full-color darkroom.

Once you have your digital image from a scanner or camera, you need to prepare it for printing on fabric. We do this by using Adobe Photoshop Elements, an inexpensive photo-editing computer program.

Photoshop offers many different ways to get the same result. There is often no right or wrong way to do something. Many high schools, colleges, and adult schools offer semester-long classes on Photoshop. In addition, book after book has been written about how to use every version of Photoshop and Photoshop Elements.

Rather than detail all the tools or techniques you can use, we have developed a simple method to quickly get great results for printing pictures on fabric. You do not need to be a computer expert to use these basic picture-processing techniques for creating unique and colorful fabric to use in your quilts.

Kerby used Photoshop Elements to combine three of his photos to create this image, *Honking at Art Quilt Tahoe*, for printing on fabric.

THE DIGITAL QUILT SYSTEM

The Digital Quilt System is a simple way to organize your work for the quickest and easiest results. It starts with the digital files of the artwork you scanned or the picture you took with your digital camera. These are your **Original files**.

From your Original image file you create a **Master file** that contains all the basic or cleanup changes you want to make. The Master file is always a copy of the Original. **Do not make any changes to an Original image file.**

There are many ways to use a picture file, and each way has its own requirements for getting the best results. Printing a picture on glossy photo paper is not the same as printing it on a piece of fabric, because the weave of the fabric reflects light differently. Coatings on papers and fabrics also change the absorption rate of the ink.

The basic principle is that you create a single Master file and from it you create many different output, or **Target files**. This way, you only need to do the work once to create your Master image.

Your output will vary depending on size and material. Some prints may be small (4″ × 6″) on glossy paper or larger on fabric. Wallpaper images on your computer, pictures on your website, and pictures sent as e-mail all have different requirements. Your Target files are where you make those adjustments to size and resolution.

> **ORIGINAL FILES** are scanned artwork or photos from your camera. Never make changes to these files.
>
> **MASTER FILES** are created from your **Original files** and contain all the basic changes needed.
>
> **TARGET FILES** are created from the **Master files** and are created for all the different ways you use an image.

SETTING UP PHOTOSHOP ELEMENTS

Menu bar →
Options bar →
Toolbar
Palette bin

This is the default screen for the Photoshop Elements Editor. It can be set up to make processing digital images easier.

There are many ways to use a program like Photoshop Elements. This is how we like to set it up.

Follow these directions to customize your Elements screen to make it easier to use. The area on the right under the Options bar is the Palette Bin.

1. Open at the top right is the Effects palette. Click on ▶▶, and uncheck Place in Palette Bin When Closed.

2. Drag the Effects palette out of the Palette Bin, and close it.

3. Open the Undo History palette: Window > Undo History. Drag the Undo History palette into the Palette Bin. Place your cursor on the bottom right corner of the Undo History box, and drag the corner to increase its size.

When you are done, the right side of your Elements screen should look like this:

The Undo History palette is one of the most useful features of Photoshop. It lets you undo your last few steps in case you make a mistake. This palette also frees you to experiment, without worrying about ruining your image.

Each change to your image is recorded in the Undo History palette in descending order. To undo a change to your image, simply click on the previous change listed above it. When you do this, notice that your last change is grayed out in the list. You can undo as many steps as are shown in the Undo History list. For example, if you back up three steps, the two below it will be grayed out. You can redo those grayed out changes by clicking on them. Once you back up and then make a new change to your image, however, all of the previous grayed-out changes will be gone.

There is one other change to make to the Elements setup to improve the color range of your picture for printing:

1. On the top menu bar in Elements, place your cursor over *Edit*. A drop-down menu will appear.

2. Click on *Color Settings* to open a dialog box.

3. Select *Always Optimize for Printing*, and click OK.

4. Now you can work on your first image.

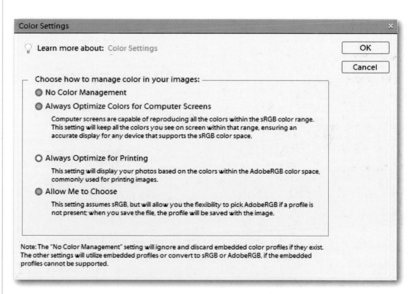

Select *Always Optimize for Printing* and click OK.

FROM ORIGINAL TO MASTER

It's so easy to take a lot of pictures with a digital camera. How you organize all those pictures on your computer is key to being able to find them and use them. A host of programs are available for sorting your pictures. Adobe Elements includes a complex Organizer program that has many options. What we use instead is a simple folder system that works for our purposes. Simply create photo folders by theme, subject, or date.

For each photo folder, you'll need to create three sub-folders: **Originals, Master**, and **Target**. These three folders are the foundation of our organizing system. Read on to see how they are used.

Whether we are shooting a JPEG or a RAW file, we refer to them as **Originals**. For these photos, create a subfolder within your photo file folder, and name the subfolder **Originals**.

WildLife folder with its subfolders: Originals, Master, and Target. (**Note:** Your screen may look different, depending on your computer and operating system.)

Some digital cameras allow you to shoot a JPEG and a RAW image file at the same time.

The JPEG image of a Canada goose is in the Originals folder. Next to it is the RAW file from a Nikon camera. The Nikon RAW file has a suffix of .NEF and does not display a thumbnail image. (**Note:** Other cameras use different suffixes.)

The first thing to do when you open a JPEG file in Photoshop Elements is to create a copy of the Original (*File > Duplicate*). Click OK in the dialog box that opens. The duplicate image of the JPEG Original has "copy" at the end of the filename and is in the foreground. Move it slightly off the Original so you can easily access the menu line of the Original; close the Original in the main window.

Never modify an Original. Who knows, in the near future, someone might create a better way to process those files. By storing the Originals, you will have the opportunity to process them with the newest, best software.

Make a duplicate, and then close the Original.

You also have the option of closing the Original in the Project Bin, which is the area at the bottom of the screen where thumbnails of open photos are displayed. Right-click on a thumbnail to close it.

If you open a RAW file, the Elements Camera Raw window opens up, which allows you to make adjustments. Once you have made any necessary adjustments, click on *Open Image* for the photo to open in the Elements Editor. Immediately create a duplicate image of the photo (*File > Duplicate*), and then **close the Original without saving any changes to it.**

A RAW file opened in the Camera Raw window. Make any changes you want, and then click on *Open Image* to get the photo into the Elements Editor.

After opening a RAW file in the Editor, make a copy, and close the Original image without saving the changes you made in the Camera Raw window.

►► Secret

Always close the Original, and work on copies.

ADJUSTING THE WHITE BALANCE

If you have the ability to shoot a RAW file, you can also adjust the White Balance (page 16) by clicking on a known gray color in the image and adjusting the picture's color.

Simply place a digital gray card (available at camera stores and online) in your scene, and shoot a picture. Then remove the gray card, and shoot the picture again. When the image with the gray card is opened in the Camera Raw window, click on the *White Balance* tool. The cursor will turn into an eyedropper. Place the eyedropper cursor on the gray card in the picture, and the color will be adjusted. For the second picture, clicking on *Basic* above the White Balance window opens a pop-up menu. Select *Previous Conversion*, and the same adjustment numbers are applied to this picture as were made to the one with the gray card.

Use the White Balance tool to adjust the color, based on the settings from a previously shot picture with a gray card.

►► continued on page 22

ADJUSTING THE WHITE BALANCE
(CONTINUED)

The important thing to remember is this: When you change lighting conditions, you need to use your gray card again. If you do not have one, look for something in your image that is about the same color of gray. Click on that part of the image with the White Balance tool.

If you are working with JPEG files that have pure black, pure white, or gray in the image, you can adjust the color in Quick Edit in the same way: Select *Enhance > Adjust Color > Remove Color Cast*. Use the eyedropper to click on the spot in the picture that has one of those three colors. The difference between this procedure and the Camera Raw procedure is that you can't save the same adjustments to another picture.

The digital gray card is still a good tool for photographers who shoot only JPEG files. Put your digital gray card in the edge of your picture to have the known color in the image so you can make the color adjustment. After making the adjustment, crop the digital gray card out of your photo.

If there is no black, white, or gray in your JPEG, go to Quick Edit, and use the Color Temperature and Tint sliders to adjust the color. Be careful when moving these sliders, as small moves can make big changes.

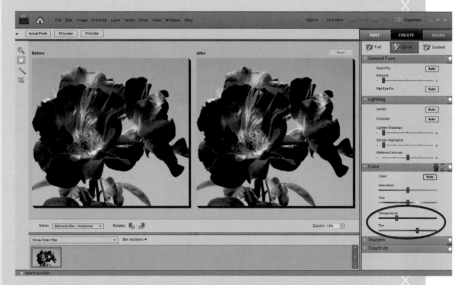

In Quick Edit, use the Temperature and Tint sliders to adjust the color of the red-and-white roses taken under incandescent light.

ROTATING AN IMAGE

If your image is not in the proper orientation, go to the *Image* drop-down menu on the top bar, and select *Rotate*. Slide across to the option you need. (This function works in either the Quick Edit or the Full Edit windows.)

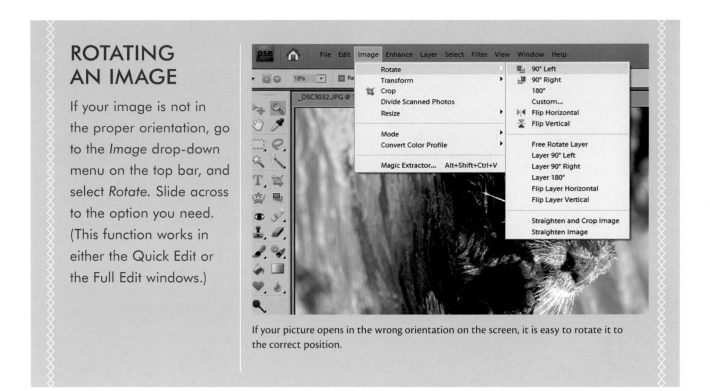

If your picture opens in the wrong orientation on the screen, it is easy to rotate it to the correct position.

EDITING YOUR MASTER FILE

Now that you've duplicated your Original image, the next step in the process is to use the Elements tools to create your Master file. After you have made all the changes you want to the Master, you will rename it and save it in a file folder labeled Master.

Photoshop Elements offers you two ways to edit your picture—either in **Full Edit** or **Quick Edit**.

The Full Edit window lets you use all the tools and menu options available in Photoshop, including adjustment layers.

Although Quick Edit can be handy, there is a very good reason for starting in Full Edit: The toolbar in Quick Edit is very limited. The first thing you'll want to do is clean your image using the Clone tool in the Full Edit toolbar.

Cleaning or Cloning Your Picture

If you scan pictures, one of the major problems is dust. No matter how much you clean the glass or wipe off the picture before you put it down, it seems that there are always dust particles on it. And these particles can be seen in your scan. Digital cameras, especially ones with interchangeable lenses, can also get dust on the photosensor. In scanned images, the dust particles are sharp. With digital camera pictures, however, the dust particles on the photosensor show up blurred in your image.

In addition to dust, there may be things in the picture that you want to get rid of, such as a leaf or twig in the wrong place, a gum wrapper, or a bright highlight.

To see these distracting items, use the Zoom tool, which is the magnifying glass in the Full Edit toolbar. Zoom the image to 100%. If there are dust spots or other items, you can easily spot them at this size.

To clean your digital image, zoom in and use the Clone tool or the Healing Brush. These tools "borrow" pixels from another part of your picture to fix the affected area.

The Clone tool copies pixels and pastes them over the other pixels, which is why the Clone icon is in the shape of a rubber stamp. The Healing Brush uses a different process to mix the pixels from one part of your image with those you want to change; its icon is a bandage.

The size of the area you are cleaning depends on the size and style of the brush you use. To select a brush type, click on the first window in the menu bar that appears when you select the tool. The second window shows the size of the brush.

For a detailed explanation of using the Clone tool, see pages 55–57.

With a clean image, you now have the choice of how to edit the picture.

Quick Editing

The Quick Edit window is unique to Photoshop Elements. It has two features not found in the full Photoshop program. One is the Before and After window, and the other is a palette of easy fixes.

To get to Quick Edit from Full Edit, click on *Quick* at the top right corner of your screen under the Edit menu.

To use either the Healing Brush or the Clone tool to clean up your picture, select the area you want to clone or heal from, using Alt-click (on a PC) or Option-click (on a Mac). You will notice a circle with cross hairs in it. This is the target area where you will pick up pixels. Move your cursor to the area where you want to paste or stamp those pixels, and click to make the change.

Click on *Quick* (at the top right of the screen) to open the Quick Edit window.

At the bottom left of the screen you will see View: After Only. Click on the drop-down menu ▼, and choose Before and After—Horizontal. You will now see changes you make in the right image in comparison to the unchanged image on the left.

If you do not see full images, go to the bottom right of the screen to adjust the zoom amount of the two pictures.

The Palette Bin allows you to make adjustments to your picture by using one of the Auto buttons or by moving individual sliders. Try all the different effects to see what they do to your image. Cancel individual changes by clicking the NO icon.

The most fun palette to use is the Color palette. In addition to using the Color sliders to correct color, you can use them to dramatically change color for effects (see pages 61–62 for examples).

With this photo, choosing Smart Fix, Levels, and Contrast made little change. Auto Color actually took color out of the picture, so the Reset button came in handy. To have some fun, we used the Color sliders instead after resetting the image.

Remember that you can undo anything by clicking the Reset button above the After image or by backing up in your Undo History when you return to Full Edit.

In the Palette Bin in the Full Edit screen, Undo History will show all the changes you made in Quick Edit. These changes are reversible by stepping back up each level.

▶▶ Secret

Quick Edit does not work on layered images. Use it when your file is a single layer. Choose Full Edit to make changes using *Layers*. For more on layers, see pages 26–28.

Using Layers

One of the most powerful aspects of Photoshop is its **Layers**, which allow you to make selective adjustments to your image, as well as to layer images as you would with a sheer fabric or a transparency. Layers can be turned on or off by clicking on the Eyeball icon in front of each layer in the Layer palette bin.

Particularly useful for printing on fabric are **Adjustment Layers**.

▶▶ Secret

The best part about using Adjustment Layers in your Master file is that you can turn them off if you need to print your image on other materials, such as glossy photo paper.

RESETTING YOUR IMAGE TO 8 BITS

JPEG images are 8-bit digital files. Other images, such as TIFF images, can be 8-bit or 16-bit digital files.

In Elements, you have more editing options with 8-bit images. If you open a 16-bit image in Full Edit some of the drop-down menus or options under the menus will be grayed out, meaning you can't use them. You also will not be able to use all of the tools in the toolbar.

▶▶ continued on page 26

RESETTING YOUR IMAGE TO 8 BITS (CONTINUED)

At the top left of the image is an information bar about the picture. If you see RGB/16 in the parentheses, then it is a 16-bit image. Change the image to 8 bit for more editing options, such as using the Clone tool or making a new Adjustment Layer.

To make the change, go to the top menu bar, select the drop-down menu under Image, and select Mode > 8 Bits/Channel. In the Undo History palette, you will see the change.

ADJUSTMENTS TO GET THE BEST COLOR ON FABRIC

LEVELS ADJUSTMENT LAYER

A **Levels Adjustment Layer** is useful for improving your picture, no matter how the final output will be used. This layer changes the brightness of your picture by changing the relationship of the information in the picture.

Layer > New Adjustment Layer > Levels opens the Levels dialog box. In the center is a graph with three small triangular sliders. The far right slider is the level of white in your picture. The far left slider is the level of black in your picture. The middle slider is where the midtones are set in your picture. A Levels adjustment affects both brightness and color at the same time. First try an Auto Levels adjustment. If you don't like the results (which can often be too dramatic), click Reset, and then click on and move the individual sliders to your taste. Check and uncheck the Preview box to see your changes before you click OK.

The new Levels layer is added to the picture in the Layers palette above the Background layer.

Making adjustments on screen may look too bright and have too much contrast. The real determination will be the fabric you are using and the type of inks in your printer. You may need to make several test prints (pages 27–28) to get it right.

BRIGHTNESS/CONTRAST ADJUSTMENT LAYER

Another adjustment layer that is very useful for printing on matte material such as fabric is **Brightness/Contrast**. Images printed on fabric benefit from increasing the brightness and contrast of the image. However, be careful not to overdo either adjustment.

There is one slider for brightness in the dialog box and a separate one for contrast. Move both sliders to the right to increase the amount of brightness and contrast. Both the image and the material you will print it on will affect the amount you want to use. It would be unusual to go more than +30 with either one.

Adjust Brightness and Contrast when printing on fabric. Adjustments should stay within the +15 to +30 range for each slider.

HUE/SATURATION ADJUSTMENT LAYER

To boost the color when printing on fabric, you can add a New Adjustment Layer for **Hue/Saturation**. Unless you want to change the color of the image, do not use the Hue slider. Boost your image's color by moving the Saturation slider to the right. This adjustment needs to be done to taste—click on and off the Preview box to see the effect. It is a good idea to make a test print (pages 27–28) after you have used the Saturation slider.

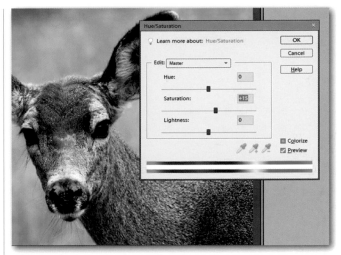

Adjusting the Saturation boosts the color.

MAKING TEST PRINTS AND ADDING TEXT

The only way to make sure that your image will print out the way you want it is to make test prints. And the best way to keep track of your test prints is to add text indicating the settings and adjustments you've made.

Adding text to a picture is easy. Choose *Image > Resize > Canvas Size* to add some canvas below your image where you can place a line of text. Increase the height of the picture slightly, and click the top center anchor arrow. It is helpful to have your rulers showing around the picture when placing text (select *View > Rulers*).

NOTE: The rulers only appear on screen; they will not appear when you print your picture.

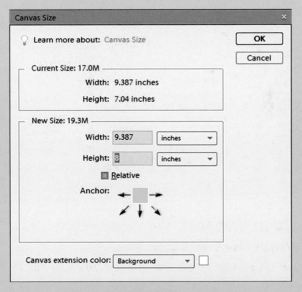

To make room for a line of text, add extra canvas to the bottom of your image. Clicking on the anchor arrows determines where the canvas will be added to your picture.

▶▶ continued on page 28

MAKING TEST PRINTS
(CONTINUED)

Click on the Text tool (uppercase T) to open the Text dialog box. This gives you options for font, style, size, color, and alignment. The Text tool also shows the Text cursor on screen. Where you click the cursor is where your line of text will start. Clicking with this cursor automatically creates a Text layer.

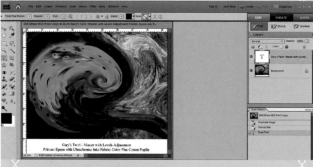

Choosing the Text tool allows you to add a line of text to your sample print.

Layers for Special Effects

Other layers can also be added to your Master file to create special effects. In *JaneAnn's Dow* (page 60), *Buster's Blues* (page 70), and *Gary's Twirl* (page 80), we show you how we used layers to create those effects.

Saving a Master Layered File

When you are finished making changes to a copy, rename it, and save it in a file folder labeled Masters. Please note that one of the changes *not* made to Master files is sharpening, because sharpening in Photoshop is best done on the final size of the Target file.

There are many formats for saving your files. Common ones are JPEGs and TIFFs. JPEGs are a compressed file format, and each time you save them, pixels are squashed. Instead, save as a TIFF, which is an uncompressed file—no pixels are damaged when the file is saved.

MASTER FILE CHECKLIST

Use this quick checklist to create each Master file after you've duplicated the Original file. Perform each step as needed.

1. Clean (page 23–24).

2. Set to 8 bits (page 25–26).

3. Add Levels Adjustment Layer (page 26).

4. Add Brightness/Contrast Adjustment Layer (page 26).

5. Add Hue/Saturation Adjustment Layer (page 27).

6. Rename, and save as a TIFF (see at left).

▶▶ Secret

Leave Master files *unsharp*. Sharpen your Target files when they are sized for printing.

FILE NAMES

The file naming system we use is Subject Picture Number MCL—for example, Blacktail 5180 MCL.tif. The subject is Blacktail, and the image number from our camera was 5180. The M at the end of the file name means Master. Since we used the Clone tool, it is now a Clean image; so we have a C in the suffix. The L means that it is a layered file. Although layered files increase the file size, they also allow you to go back later and reverse or change any adjustments you made to the image in that layer.

TARGET FILES

You may have many different uses for a Master file. Because each use may be different, you should create individual print files in a folder called Target files. The most common types of Target files are based on the final size of the print. Some common print sheet sizes are 8½″ × 11″, 13″ × 19″, and 17″ × 22″. In addition to Target files for multiple print sizes, you may choose to have Target files for printing with different printers or for different uses, such as websites and e-mail.

Before you make your first Target file, make a copy of the Master file to work on, because your Master file is now an original Master. Since you may make many different Target files from your Master, you don't want to take any chances on changing it.

Duplicate your Master file in the same way you duplicated your Original images: Make a copy of your Master, and close the original Master file.

Flattening Your File

After you have closed your original Master file and are working on your copy, the first thing to do is flatten it by selecting *Layer > Flatten Image*. Flattening your copy makes the file smaller and takes up less storage room on your computer. Other adjustments, such as resizing the image, go faster with smaller files.

Resizing the Picture

To make your image the correct size for printing—for instance, when you are using an 8½″ × 11″ paper-backed fabric sheet—you will need to resize it.

From the menu bar, select *Image > Resize > Image Size*. In the Image Size dialog box, change the resolution to the same as your printer. For example, for Epson printers, use 360 ppi; for other printers, use 300 ppi. To change the resolution without changing the file size, be sure the Resample Image box at the bottom of the dialog box is unchecked and the three boxes labeled Width, Height, and Resolution are linked.

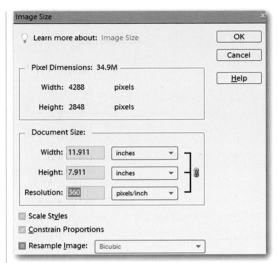

In this example, the resolution is changed to that for an Epson pigmented ink print of 360 ppi.

After you have set the resolution for your printer, you need to set the size for printing. Check the Resample Image box so that only the Width and Height boxes are linked.

Clicking the Resample Image box brings up a drop-down menu ▼ in which the first option is *Bicubic*. This refers to the process that the software uses for removing pixels in the picture to make it smaller or larger. When making the image smaller, some feel that *Bicubic Sharper* works best. If a picture is being sized up, the general recommendation is to use *Bicubic Smoother*. This is all fine-tuning; if you forget to change the box, the default *Bicubic* works fine.

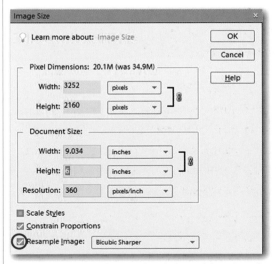

Checking the Resample Image box links Width and Height. In this example, the size of the print is changed to 6″ × 9″, and the Resolution remains constant at 360 ppi.

Adjust the width and height for your desired output. Then click OK.

What if your image won't naturally resize to your desired output? For instance, a good size for an image on 8½″ × 11″ fabric sheets is 7″ × 9½″. Another size that is not standard but useful is 6″ × 9″. If your image won't naturally resize to the dimensions you want, leave the height and width unchanged, and click OK. Now you are back to the Full Edit window, where you can crop the image to your desired size.

Cropping

Cropping is another manipulation that you can do in either Quick Edit or Full Edit. We recommend that you do **not** crop your Master file unless you are absolutely sure there is something that you do not want in it. Once a picture is cropped and saved, you have thrown away that part of the picture; therefore, the place to crop a picture is the Target file.

On the left side of the screen is the Photoshop Elements toolbar. The Quick Edit toolbar has only four icons. Click on the fourth icon: the Crop tool.

With your mouse or touchpad, move the Crop cursor to the place on the picture where you want to start the crop. Click and hold, dragging the guide to where you want to finish the crop.

A box with blinking dashes appears with eight drag points; some people refer to the dashes as racing or marching ants. The image outside of the blinking dashes is dimmed down.

You can use your keyboard's arrow or your mouse to move this box around the image. You can also make the crop area smaller or larger by dragging on one of the eight anchor points. If you entered an aspect ratio or specific size (see at right) in the crop guide window, the box will maintain its proportions as you drag. If you did not, you can change the shape of the box.

To crop the picture, click on the checkmark icon at the bottom right of the box, or simply press Enter on your keyboard. If you want to cancel the crop and start over, click on the No icon below the picture.

Cropping a photo using the Crop tool in Full Edit mode.

When you choose the Crop tool, a window appears in which you can enter a predetermined size for your crop. On the top toolbar are four windows labeled Aspect Ratio, Width, Height, and Resolution.

In the Aspect Ratio window, you can select a standard ratio, such as 5 × 7. If you want a custom size, enter numbers such as 7.5 in the Width window and 9 in the Height window. When you enter a number, the Aspect Ratio window will automatically change to Custom.

An easy change is to reverse the orientation of your crop from vertical to horizontal—just click on the two arrows between the Width and Height windows, and the numbers will reverse. This keeps the same size crop, but changes the orientation from horizontal to vertical and back to horizontal.

Depending on the size and the quality that you want, you can set the resolution when you make the crop. We suggest that you use either 180 or 360 ppi for Epson printers and 150 or 300 ppi for other printers.

To maintain a particular size, known as Aspect Ratio, when you are cropping, look at the Options bar below the Menu bar.

Sharpening

There are many ways to sharpen a picture. For fabric, I like to use **more** sharpening than I use for a paper print because of the weave of the material. I could use the Auto Sharpen tool in Quick Edit, but I actually prefer to choose *Unsharp Mask* in the Full Edit window. This option is located under the *Enhance* menu on the top bar (on older versions of Elements, this option may be in the *Filters* drop-down menu).

You can only get to the Unsharp Mask dialog box after you have flattened your picture (page 29). The sliders available in this window are Amount and Radius. Use the Amount slider to taste, and check it by clicking and unclicking the Preview box to see the effect. You can click and drag within the window to view various areas of the picture and click on the − and + to zoom in or out.

A caution on the Radius slider: Do not go over 1 pixel, or it will start to look unreal.

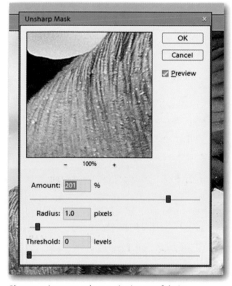

Sharpen images when printing on fabric.

Saving Your Target File

Once you have sharpened your image, save and rename your Master Layered Copy file as a Target file.

The file name suffix changes from MCL to MCS. The layers are gone, and so is the L. The S indicates that you sharpened it. And the 8x4-2 indicates the size of the picture in inches.

Save the file in your Target folder, and use the naming convention Honker 3833 MCS 8x4-2.tif.

> ▶▶ Secret
>
> We use a dash instead of a period to indicate 4.2 inches. Periods are only used before formats such as tif or jpg. If you use a period in the number, the computer will expect to see a format suffix. If it sees a 2 after the period, it will not know what type of file it is and will not be able to open it.

PRINTING YOUR TARGET FILE

Once you think you have your Target file ready for printing, make a test print. If your supply of laminated fabric sheets is small, you can make a test print on a piece of plain paper. Since plain paper is matte, it will give you an idea of what your image will look like on fabric.

If the result is not as good as you think it should be, check your printer's manual to see if you can adjust the settings for better results. Always choose the best print quality. It may be a bit slower printing, but the color will be much better.

When reading the printer's manual, look for the Advanced Settings dialog boxes, where you can change settings from default ones that give you only sRGB color to the setting for the larger color space of AdobeRGB (see page 14).

If you get washed-out color or you see bands across the printed image, then your printer may need to have its head(s) cleaned. Your printer's manual should include a section on utilities, which will tell you how to clean and align your printer's head(s).

Experiment with the printer's paper source setting. We have never found a setting for fabric on any of the printers we have owned. But you can find settings for different types of papers, such as matte papers and fine art papers, that may give you better results than leaving the setting on automatic.

It is also a good idea to take one of your typical images and run it through your printer with a variety of different settings. Use the Text tool (page 27) to make notes on the settings in the picture's margin. This makes it easy to make comparisons side by side and to remember which settings gave you the best results.

▸▸ Secret

Save both your Master and Target files as TIFFs.

PHOTO BY C&T PUBLISHING

Hawaiian Ferns—Lawae, 51″ × 38″, by Joan Davis, 2007.

This quilt started with a digital photo Joan Davis took of ferns in a Maui garden.

punch it up

Bee Bop, 33″ × 37″, by Lura Schwarz Smith, 2008.

Some of the digital fabric used in Bee Bop was enhanced with textile markers and inking techniques.

ADDING SURFACE DESIGN MATERIALS TO ENHANCE YOUR FABRICS

Why should you enhance your fabrics with added surface design materials? Even the most beautifully printed digital fabrics can benefit from a little boost. Or sometimes the fabric prints are not quite as vivid as you might wish, or the texture of the fabric might obscure fine details. This can be brought into focus with easily applied art materials. Adding line, shading, and color can add interest and a unique, artistic look. Using these materials on both digital and other fabrics integrates them. And best of all, it's just plain fun to draw, paint, and ink on fabric.

This is a portrait of Father Christmas as it came out of an Epson printer using pigmented inks.

Lura used inks, markers, and colored pencils to punch up this digital fabric print of Father Christmas.

The following are some of Lura's favorite art materials for use on fabrics. There are always interesting new materials to try. When in doubt, test it—it may work just fine and give you a wonderful new effect.

PERMANENT AND WASHABLE WHEN HEAT SET:

- Tsukineko All-Purpose Inks and Fantastix Applicators

- Textile paints: Pebeo Setacolor; Liquitex Soft Body Acrylics; Jacquard Textile, Lumiere, and Neocolor Paints; Versatex Screen Printing Ink

- Shiva Paintstiks

- Marking pens: Fabrico; Pebeo Setascrib; Y & C FabricMate; Faber Castell Pitt Artist's Markers; Pigma Microns

- Sakura Gelly Roll Pens

- Pentel Fabric Fun Oil Pastel Dye Sticks

SUITABLE FOR TEXTILE WALL ART (NOT WASHABLE):

- Soluble oil pastels and crayons: Caran d'Ache Neocolor II; Portfolio; Lyra Aquacolor; Loew Cornell Aqua Crayon Sticks

- Watercolor-colored pencils: various brands

- Prismacolor Colored Pencils

- Crayola Crayons

Washable or Wall Art?

An important factor in choosing your art materials is washability. Will your finished project be hung on the wall, or will it need to be colorfast when washed? Optimally, for projects using digital fabrics, you will not be laundering your finished project. The digital fabrics fade somewhat if washed, even with pigmented inks, especially with repeated washings. The good news is that the fact that these should not be washed gives you a much wider range of options for added surface design materials—many of which are brilliant and beautiful on fabrics but are not washable. For any project not using digital fabrics that you do plan to launder, washability is an important factor.

NOTE: Some of these materials tested very well in the single gentle cycle QuiltWash test (see at right), but there was some color loss. This fading would continue with repeated washings. Unless a substance holds true color and vibrancy with repeated laundering, it isn't truly washable. There are good options for those projects that require true permanence and washability.

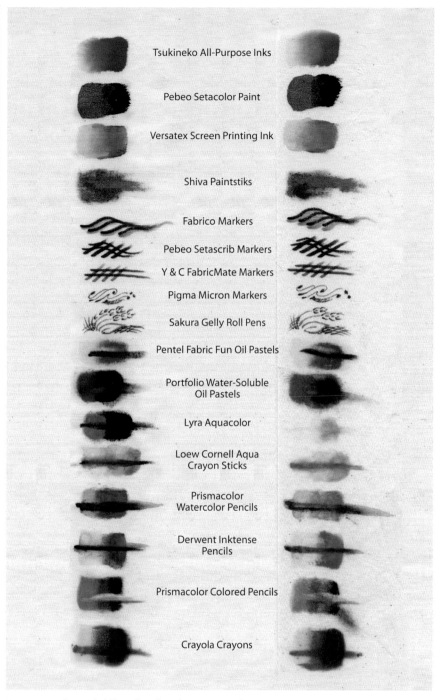

Tsukineko All-Purpose Inks

Pebeo Setacolor Paint

Versatex Screen Printing Ink

Shiva Paintstiks

Fabrico Markers

Pebeo Setascrib Markers

Y & C FabricMate Markers

Pigma Micron Markers

Sakura Gelly Roll Pens

Pentel Fabric Fun Oil Pastels

Portfolio Water-Soluble Oil Pastels

Lyra Aquacolor

Loew Cornell Aqua Crayon Sticks

Prismacolor Watercolor Pencils

Derwent Inktense Pencils

Prismacolor Colored Pencils

Crayola Crayons

To compare the washability of surface design materials, we made two sample testers: before washing (left) and after washing with QuiltWash in cold water, gentle cycle (right).

Lightfast and Fade Resistant

We know that most fabrics fade when exposed to direct sunlight or bright light. If you protect your quilts from light as much as possible, the fade resistance of these art materials is sufficient with usual care of the quilt.

The Dot Test for Bleeding

When using wet media, choosing the right fabrics will make the process much more successful. The digital fabric prints you create should be tested as well, as these may vary and it's important to know what you have to work with. For other fabrics, you have more choice in the matter. Fabrics vary widely in their resistance to bleeding. Finding fabrics that do not bleed will allow you to put your mark where you want it to go—and have it stay there!

Because the greige or base fabrics can change even with known fabric lines, get in the habit of testing each fabric before you buy or use it, even if it is a fabric you have used before. We call this test the Dot Test.

Use a textile marker with a medium tip, such as a Fabrico marker. (**Note:** Sakura Pigma Microns have too small a tip for an accurate test.) Place the blunt tip on the fabric surface, and count slowly to 5. Lift the marker. What you want is a nice, clean dot the size of the marker tip. If you see ink haloing out from the marker tip, that fabric will bleed. Take the marker with you to fabric shops, and ask for the tiniest snip or edge to test. A little bleed is okay; as you test, you will see how results vary. Remember, what you are looking for with the Dot Test is a nice, crisp little freckle about the size of your marker tip, not a big fuzzy mole.

> ▶▶ **Secret**
>
> Don't use all-purpose markers on fabric! A Sharpie or other permanent nontextile marker will bleed badly on any fabric, have a strong odor, and leave a chemical residue. Permanent textile markers are washable but follow the manufacturer's guidelines as all markers differ.

TSUKINEKO INKS AND FANTASTIX APPLICATORS

Tsukineko All-Purpose Inks are transparent and blendable until heat set, and then they are permanent. Each color of ink has two Fantastix applicators—a blunt tip and a brush (pointed) tip. All blending can be done directly on the fabrics. The inks are very versatile—each color ranges from brilliant, intense tones right down to the palest of pastels, depending on how it is applied.

> ▶▶ **Secret**
>
> Number your Fantastix and your inks with the ink number to keep them paired and easy to use. Custom stands make this much easier (see Resources, page 94).

The blunt tip is best for blending two colors with full intensity. Dip only the foam tip, and ink a smooth, streak-free area on a piece of fabric. Next, take another color blunt-tip Fantastix, dip briefly, and blend it into the first color. You can reapply the first color again if desired, and with the blunt tips, you can rub the colors together for blending. Keep a piece of practice muslin nearby as your rub cloth to check how much ink is in the Fantastix and to rub off excess ink.

Blend rich colors with the blunt-tip Fantastix.

The pointed brush tip Fantastix works best for pastel dry brush applications, as there is less material in the tapering point, so the ink rubs out faster. Briefly dip the whole tip into your ink. Hold the Fantastix so it is tipped a bit to the side and the whole angle of the tapered tip touches the fabric. This way you will cover more area with each stroke. Gently rub the Fantastix back and forth without lifting it. As the ink is rubbed out onto the fabric, the color will lighten more and more. Make long color strip exercises in smooth gradients. Keep practicing until you get a smooth, streak-free, pale pastel area. This is the most important part of the learning curve—rubbing enough ink out of the applicator so shading is controllable. Once you master this step, it's just like using a colored pencil or crayon.

Add one delicate tone over another to get subtle color blending right on the fabric. Always test the amount of ink in the Fantastix on your rub cloth first.

Practice the color strip exercise with brush tip Fantastix until you can get controllable pastel tones for shading.

MARKING PENS FOR TEXTILES

Use textile markers for line and detail work and for small areas of intense punch. Tsukineko's Fabrico Textile Markers have dual tips, blunt and brush, and come in a wide range of colors. Like the inks, these are blendable until heat set, so press before using with other colors if you don't want a blend. Once heat set, they are permanent and washable.

Another brand is Setascrib, made by Pebeo. These are larger markers, but the tips taper to a fine point. FabricMate markers by Yasutomo offer basic and pastel colors in a brush tip. For finest line and detail, Sakura Pigma Micron markers come in a range of six fine-line widths. Though not marketed specifically as textile markers, some art markers may also work. Faber Castell Pitt Artist's Markers have no chemical odor, are washable, and come in blunt and small brush tips in beautiful subtle colors.

Bee Bop (full quilt on page 33)

Detail and emphasis were added to the digitally printed bees with Fabrico markers

TEXTILE PAINTS

Pebeo Setacolor paints; Liquitex Soft Body Acrylics; Jacquard Textile, Neocolor, and Lumiere paints; and Versatex Screen Printing Inks are excellent textile paints. Though labeled inks, Versatex is like an acrylic paint in consistency, so don't be misled by the label. These brands are water soluble and can be used right out of the bottle for heavier applications, thinned with water, or used with their clear extenders. The Setacolors come in transparent, opaque, and shimmer colors. Jacquard paints include fluorescent, metallic, and pearlescent colors.

Be cautious in applying extremely heavy applications of paint, as this could cause difficulties in the quilting process. Try using various brushes for different effects.

Sunflower II, 12" × 13", by Lura Schwarz Smith, 2005.

This quilt was enhanced with Versatex Screen Printing Ink.

PAINT STICKS

Shiva's Paintstik is one of several good brands of paint sticks. These sticks are oil paint in solid form, like a crayon. They are quite dense and not for detail work, but they work well for texture rubbings and areas of bold emphasis. A self-healing film forms over the tip after each use. Available in regular and iridescent, these sticks are permanent once dried and can be heat set according to manufacturer's instructions.

> ▶▶ Secret
>
> If you use artists' acrylic paints on your fabrics, try mixing them with Golden GAC 900 Fabric Medium or Liquitex Fabric Medium to help soften and blend the acrylics for a better hand and permanence on fabric.

GEL ROLL PENS

For the finest lines and details, waterproof archival gel roll pens are excellent. The Sakura Gelly Roll Pens are especially nice and come in fine and medium points and in opaque, metallic, and glitter colors. These pens are also wonderful for cursive writing on labels—they roll smoothly and don't catch in the fibers on upstrokes, as the finest-point Microns can.

TEXTILE OIL PASTELS

Pentel Oil Pastel Dye Sticks are like artist's oil pastels, but they are specially formulated for textiles and are permanent once heat set. They come in a range of 15 colors and are bright and blendable. Though not a detail tool, these dye sticks are good for bold strokes and forms. Being opaque, they can add lighter colors and highlights over darker colors. Another great use is to do rubbings with water-soluble oil pastels or paint sticks over textured surfaces, such as wood, stone, brick, or concrete.

PHOTO BY LURA SCHWARZ SMITH

A digital fabric print is boosted with Pentel Fabric Fun Oil Pastels rubbed over rough wood to add texture, color, and value to the stone images.

▶▶ Secret

Use inks, markers, and gel roll pens **before** using oily or waxy substances (e.g., oil pastels, crayons, paint sticks), so the pen and marker tips will not get clogged by the oils.

WATER-SOLUBLE OIL PASTELS AND CRAYONS

Though not washable, water-soluble oil pastels and crayons are wonderful additions to wall art pieces. They are rich, vivid, and great fun to use by applying and then brushing with water or by dipping them into water and applying wet. They can also be used dry. Caran d'Ache Neocolor II comes in a wide range of colors and gives an especially creamy, rich color application. Portfolio and Lyra are also good brands. Special care needs to be taken with heat setting these brands when used without water. Allow to dry for at least 24 hours, and use a pressing cloth to avoid any pigment migration.

WATERCOLOR PENCILS

Watercolor pencils work in much the same way as water-soluble oil pastels, but they give more detail. Prismacolor, Faber Castell, Derwent Inktense, Caran d'Ache, and others are available. They are not washable, but they are stable once heat set.

PRISMACOLOR COLORED PENCILS

These richly pigmented pencils have wonderful applications on fabrics. They are excellent for tracing, for adding highlights and lighter colors over darker, and for shading, especially in small areas. Though advertised as permanent and waterproof, they do not launder well. However, they are fade resistant and are great fun to use.

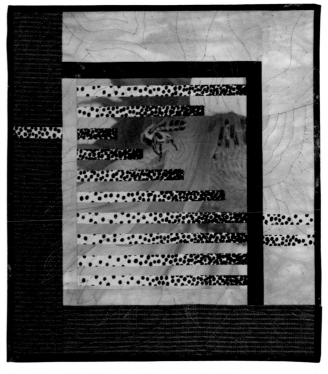

Honey Lime, 15″ × 17″, by Lura Schwarz Smith, 2007.

Prismacolor pencils and Fabrico markers add zest.

CRAYOLA CRAYONS

This humble product has a wide array of beautiful colors with surprisingly vivid results on fabric, though they are not truly washfast. Heat set them by using paper as a pressing cloth to remove the wax. Heavy applications can leave fabric stiff.

NOTE: Washable Crayola Crayons are formulated to wash out, which is not desirable for our purposes. Crayola Fabric Crayons come in only eight colors and are for transfer onto synthetic fabrics.

Shore Memories, 8″ × 40″, by Genie Becker, 2008.

Enhanced with crayons and ink

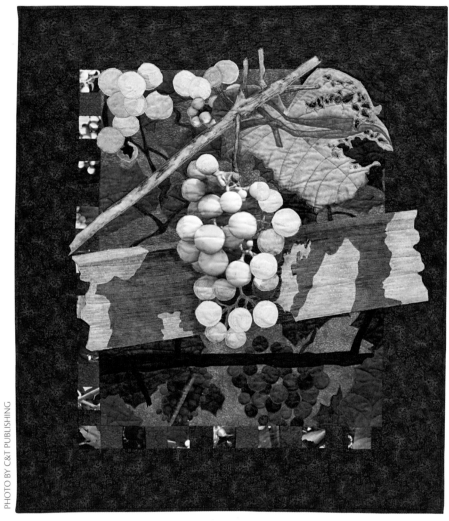

Finger Lakes Bounty, 37″ × 43″, by Caren Betlinski, 2008.

Enhanced with Tsukineko Inks

put it all together

Il Postino, 17″ × 16″, by Lura Schwarz Smith, 2008.

This quilt uses Lura's free-form machine piecing and combines digital and traditional fabrics.

Whether you like to plan your project carefully or work it out by happy accident as the project evolves, it is helpful to keep the basic elements of design in mind. For assembly, free-form machine piecing, fusing, and machine or hand appliqué give us plenty of options.

A NEW KID IN THE STASH

You add an exciting element of potential to your art quilts with digital fabrics as the new kid in the stash. Now what? You have florals, plaids, stripes, solids—and now, digital fabrics. Like many other textile prints, digital fabrics tend to have a specific look. That's the good news and the bad news—this distinctive look can be a focal point, but it can also be overpowering if not used with attention.

Dusk, 17″ × 16″, by Lura Schwarz Smith, 2006.

Digital fabrics are a part of the background elements rather than forming the main imagery.

DESIGN BASICS

Working with quilt patterns gives you a basic structure, but in creating original art quilts, you must do more. As in any art form, your goal is to fill the space in an interesting way, using the elements and principles of design to engage and move the eye across the surface. Design can be a complex subject, but a basic understanding gives you powerful tools to help create exciting art pieces. The following photographs show some examples of how to use these elements, which can be applied to the process of designing art quilts.

Positive and Negative Spaces

PHOTO BY GARY SMITH

Cropping in tightly can create interesting shapes that are intentionally cut off, engaging the edges, as in this photo of a hay hook.

PHOTO BY LURA SCHWARZ SMITH

The negative space, or the space between and around objects, can be a very important part of the composition. This shot of a canal and bridge in Burano, Italy uses the negative space as the primary focus.

Creating Depth

PHOTO BY LURA SCHWARZ SMITH

Overlapping objects help create a sense of depth.

PHOTO BY LURA SCHWARZ SMITH

Converging lines of the fence and stone wall at the left and a diminishing scale of objects in the distance give depth to a composition, as in this scene near Newgrange, Ireland.

Symmetry and Balance

This photo shows a Tuscany street scene with a symmetrical composition. Symmetry gives a strong, stable system of balance.

PHOTO BY LURA SCHWARZ SMITH

A close-up of a mantis on a rose is deliberately off-center in an asymmetrical composition.

Shape and Form

Growing roses in deer country is our delight. The repetitive curving shapes of the petals in this Double Delight rose create a rhythm with the echoing forms.

Strong curved and straight lined forms show an interesting contrast of shapes in this Charleston street scene.

A fish-eye lens adds an element of distortion in this interplay between the contrasting repetitive shapes of the massive columns of ruins at the Roman Coliseum and the hastening tourists below.

Focal Points

PHOTO BY LURA SCHWARZ SMITH

For a contrast in scale at Cannon Beach, Oregon, a human figure stands near the large monolith, with reflections shimmering in the wet sand.

PHOTO BY GARY SMITH

Diagonal placement of the hens contrasts with the grid pattern of the wire, with the hens' red combs providing a focus.

Line: Defining Form and Adding Movement

Lines create form and texture in the metal sculptures at the Getty Center, Los Angeles.

Slender curving branches of a Silversword plant high on Haleakela, Maui, create a graceful, linear movement and mood.

Texture: Pattern, Repeats, and Rich Surfaces

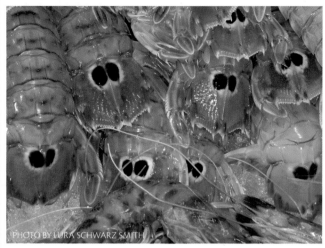

A Venice street fish market shows varying crustacean textures.

Prehistoric carvings at Newgrange, Ireland, provide repeats and changing texture. Smaller stones and grass give contrast texture.

Solstice Stars at the Cabin (quilt on page 92); group quilt by Lura Schwarz Smith, Betty Robinson, Betty Tikker Davis, Betty Magan, Donna Butts, and Sharon Hebrard, quilted by Kelly Gallagher Abbott, 2007.

Fabric prints provide texture, and the quilting adds another linear physical texture.

Complementary colors are opposites on the color wheel and can have a big punch with high contrast, as in this ti leaf plant on Maui.

COLOR: A RAINBOW OF POSSIBILITIES

Becoming familiar with the color wheel and how to use various color schemes gives you powerful tools for designing your textile art. Color temperature (warm or cool), saturation (intensity), value (dark and light), and tints (adding white) and shades (adding black) to colors allow for great subtleties and endless possibilities of combinations. Color is a tremendously important and fun subject. Here are a few examples of color usage.

PHOTO BY LURA SCHWARZ SMITH

Muted complementary colors give less intense contrast with these boys kayaking on Scotts Flat Lake in Nevada City, California.

▶▶ TIP

There are many good books on color theory and use. An excellent one, with detailed applications of color theory for textile use, is *Design Explorations for the Creative Quilter* by Katie Pasquini Masopust (see Resources, page 94).

This interior wide-angle, fish-eye lens, shot at the Vatican Museum in Rome, combines warm tones above with the cool tones below.

The primary colors of red, blue, and yellow make a strong, contrasting statement.

Using a range of a single color is a monochromatic color scheme, as in these rocks on our property in the Sierra Nevadas.

This iris glows with a range of warm analogous colors, which are next to each other on the color wheel.

Value: Dark and Light

High contrast in values (from very light to very dark) produces a dramatic effect, as in this street scene late in the day in Cortona, Italy.

Color values in a closer range are subtler and can be just as effective as high-contrast images, as in these roses from our garden.

CONSTRUCTION TECHNIQUES

Raindrops, 18″ × 14″, by Lura Schwarz Smith, 2007.

Raindrops is fused, layering a digital cloud fabric and the cut-apart sunflower detail with other fabrics.

Fusing and Fabric Adhesives

Fusing is a good choice when layering images with detailed, complex edges. You can cut out your image exactly the way you want it to be outlined. This technique has the advantage of being fast, direct, and very freeing in many ways. On the other hand, it does not work well over piecing, as the pieced seam underneath will cause a ridge. This seam can be dealt with to some extent by trimming away the pieced layers below, but that is a lot of work, and the edges of the seam will still show at the underlap area. Even other fused layers can cause tiny ridges, and fusing too many layers can be challenging to machine quilt. Most fusibles are too stiff to hand quilt comfortably, though Misty Fuse is so delicate that it can be hand quilted, especially if it is used with fine or sheer fabrics.

Once fused, outline stitching, a tiny zigzag stitch, or machine quilting can be used to secure the fused pieces.

Imagine (full quilt on page 75)

Free-motion stitching close to the edges attaches fused digital fabric.

Fabric spray adhesives, such as Sulky KK 2000 and Formula 505 Spray and Fix, may be used for temporarily attaching fabrics in the assembly process. Spray in a well-ventilated area, as the fumes are strong.

Music for the Soul, 8½″ × 11″, by Lura Schwarz Smith, 2004.

Digital images of roses combine with other fabrics and the inked hands. Machine quilting and tiny zigzag stitches attach the fused fabrics.

Hand and Machine Appliqué

Hand appliqué is a time-honored technique. It gives a clean, smooth edge without visible stitches, if your stitches are tiny and well placed. For needle-turn appliqué, cut out your image, leaving approximately ⅛″ edge to turn under. Pin the appliqué shape onto the top, and use a thread that matches the appliqué edge color. Hand appliqué works well over a pieced background, which can easily be trimmed away on the underside if needed.

Machine appliqué can be used over a pieced or layered area. Cut out the form precisely, as in fusing, and pin it to the quilt top. Use a satin or zigzag stitch to apply. For raw-edge work, attach the appliqué with a straight stitch, leaving a small amount of raw edge for fraying.

Free-Form Machine Curved Piecing: P-Free!

This kind of piecing is called P-Free because it uses No Paper, No Pins, and, for many uses, No Planning. It's just fast and free rotary cutting fun. This kind of free-form piecing is easiest with fairly shallow curves. But with practice, deeper curves and even angles can be achieved. Even without deep curves, beautiful and interesting textures, forms, and a sense of depth can quickly be created by stacking and crossing these cuts.

NO PAPER

A simple curve is like a flattened-out C shape. A countercurve has a reversal, like a flattened-out S shape. Try combinations and variations of these cuts. The following simple exercise shows how to get an overlap effect, such as in a tuft of grass with one blade in front of another.

1. Choose 3 fabrics: A for the background, B for the back blade of grass, and C for the front blade of grass. Make C, the front fabric, the most dominant in order to increase the effect of depth.

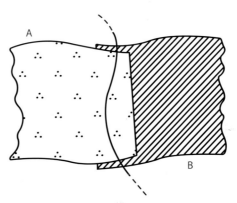

Overlap A and B fabrics about 12″ long, right sides up. Make the overlap about 3″ to 4″ wide to allow for your curving cut.

2. Use a rotary cutter to make a free-form, shallow S-shaped curve across both fabrics within the overlap area. Remove the excess pieces so that you have two different fabrics meeting perfectly, with no gaps and no overlaps in your cut. If necessary, re-layer your fabrics, and make a new cut. Note that the pair of fabrics that you removed will also meet and make an opposite pair.

3. If desired, use a textile marking pen or chalk pencil to make a registration mark across the two fabrics where they meet in several places, keeping within the space of your ¼″ seam allowance. This step is optional but can be comforting if you are new to free curved piecing.

NO PINS

1. Place A and B right sides together. Note that now the curves in your two fabrics do not meet at all. **Resist pinning.** It does take strength of character not to pin, but it truly is much easier to let the countercurves fall freely at this point. Just align the first ½″ of your fabrics where your seam will go so that both fabrics will feed evenly under the presser foot, and begin your seam. Use the needle-down position if your machine has the option.

2. As you stitch using a ¼″ seam allowance, gently bring the curved fabrics together in a scissoring move, so that the two fabrics line up with each other just as they go under the presser foot. Do not pull forward or back, as this stretches the biases and can add ripples and bulges. Just gently bring the two fabrics together as they move under the presser foot. Sometimes the convex curve will be on top, sometimes the concave curve; gently scissor both curves in so they align with each other as you stitch.

> **NOTE:** If you made registration marks, do not stretch the biases to make them meet, as that will create fullness and ripples at the seam. Just notice if they do not meet, and stitch without stressing biases. If necessary, use the Curve Correction technique.

3. When the seam is finished, press the entire seam to one side. If it flips midway, a bump in the curve will result. Check to see that your seam is smooth and that both pieces of fabric lie flat. Most curves will not require clipping unless they are very deep.

4. Layer another fabric A right side up over your AB seamed unit. You can precut a curve or place one of the cutaway pieces to get ideas. Either way, make sure that your second cut crosses the first seam. Remove the excess, but do not throw it out—you can bring it back into the project later. Stitch, press the new seam all to one side, and check that the entire project lies flat.

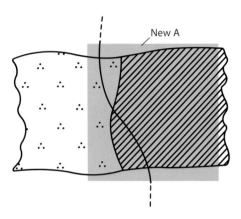

Overlap background fabric A on the right, and make another cut across the AB unit. Seam and press.

▶▶ Secret

For more interesting shapes, vary the length, shape, and curve of your cuts. Resist trimming the P-Free project into straight edges as you work. This technique builds form in an organic way and gives projects a free-form look.

▶▶ Secret

After pressing a seam, if there is a slight lip of excess fabric at the seam:

1. Make sure the whole project lies flat.

2. Press fullness toward the seam firmly.

3. Open and restitch along the new press line.

This Curve Correction technique invisibly eliminates the missed curve lip.

5. Place fabric C right side up for your next cut, which will cross over the ABA unit. Make the free curving cut, continuing through all fabrics completely. Remove the excess pieces, saving the cutaways. Stitch and press the new seam to one side.

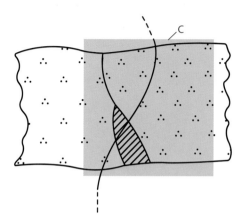

Overlap fabric C on the right, and cut across the ABA unit midway, leaving enough of the unit on both sides of the cut (the split) to reconnect. Stitch and press the new seam to one side.

6. Place the cutaway ABA section of the unit on the new unit to give the effect of one blade crossing in front of another. This is the split; the insertion of the C fabric gives that effect. Follow the cutaway shape with a new cut through all layers. Stitch and press the seam to one side.

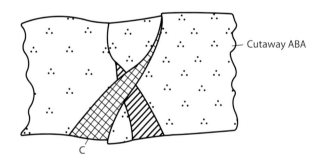

Fabric C now appears to pass in front of A and B, giving a sense of depth with the overlap.

NO PLANNING

Continue free cutting and piecing for more complex units: make the new cut, stitch, and press. Working freely and abstractly without a plan can result in wonderful surprises, like tiny shapes formed by reseaming earlier cutaway units. For some projects, planning can be added of course, but working Plan Free is a great way to loosen up and really learn the possibilities of curved free piecing.

Sikiel: Angel of the Sirocco (full quilt on page 5)

This detail shows free piecing; the quilt is appliquéd only at the front of the profile, around the hand, and on the lower legs. Digital fabric was used only in the background.

Tomato Swirl, 21″ × 18½″,
by Ingrid Cattaneo, 2008.

My Orchid, 13¼″ × 11⅜″,
by Patricia E. Nelson, 2008.

step out
of the frame

Honeymoon 1944, 34" × 38", by Lura Schwarz Smith, 2008.

MAKING A MEMORABLE MEMORY QUILT

Lura's mother, Maudie, was always a photo bug. She loved taking pictures, especially family pictures. She used a variety of simple, inexpensive cameras over the years, and the pictures that were not in albums filled old shoeboxes and drawers. In her 90s now, she doesn't take many pictures, but she still loves looking at them.

Looking through her photo boxes, we found pictures and postcards from Maudie and Emmette's honeymoon in 1944. We decided to scan them and print them on fabric so Lura could make a memory wall quilt for her mother. Adding drawn and inked hands caught in the act of pinning these photos to a bulletin board was Lura's idea to give this memory quilt extra dimension and personalization. Kerby tackled the first part of the team project: preparing and printing the digital fabric photos.

MATERIALS

> NOTE: This project offers guidelines and techniques for creating your own unique photo project rather than specifics for an exact replica of our project. Select materials as appropriate for your project.

Scans of old photos

Prepared fabric sheets

Background fabric

Muslin or skin-tone fabric, nonbleed (see page 36)

Fusible web (optional, if desired for construction)

Fabrics for backing and binding

Batting

OPTIONAL FOR CREATING HAND-INKED HANDS:
Transparency film sheets (used on overhead projectors)

Sharpie Ultra-Fine black marker

Prismacolor pencils

Tsukineko All-Purpose inks and Fantastix applicators

Scanning and Printing Your Images

GETTING THE BEST SCANS FROM OLD FAMILY PHOTOS

- **Scan the best print.** Various drugstores, supermarkets, and camera stores often give a bonus set of prints. One set usually goes in the photo album. Over time, those pictures might suffer from handling, be cracked or dog-eared, or have jam dropped on them. The second set usually remains in the original envelope with the negatives. Check those old photo envelopes to make sure you have the best print before scanning it.

- **Clean the glass on the scanner.** Smudges and dirt on the glass of the scanner will show up in your pictures.

- **Scan at the largest size you want to use.** Instead of scanning a 3″ × 5″ print at its original size and blowing it up in Elements, scan it at the size you want to print it. Scanning to the output size means you have more information and a sharper image to work with when you take it into Elements.

- **Save scans as TIFFs.** You want the best file with the most pixels to work on to create your Master file (page 23). The TIFF format is an uncompressed format that gives you the most pixels to work with when editing your picture.

- **Scan black and white as color.** When you scan a black-and-white photo as a color image, you have more flexibility in how you process it in Elements.

SCANNING NOTES

All the postcards and photo prints were scanned at 200%. Scanning a print at original size and enlarging it in Elements results in the computer program having to make pixels to fill in. However, by scanning the photograph at 200%, every pixel is recording information from the original print. The size of the Target file (page 29) is the same regardless of the method used, but the quality of the pixels that make up the file are different. This was especially important for the written side of the postcards.

One of the special things that told the story of Maudie's honeymoon trip were the written postcards she sent home to her family. By scanning and printing at 200%, we made sure the words from 1944 could be read clearly.

Be sure to leave a little white space for seam allowances around each image you scan. When setting the scanner resolution for your image file, match it to the resolution of your printer (pages 7–8). If you are using an HP printer with a native resolution of 300 ppi, set the scan resolution for 300 ppi. Because we planned to print the old photos and postcards on an Epson printer, we set the scanner resolution to 360 ppi.

▶▶Secret

If you have two or more printers with different native resolutions, scan for the printer that has the higher native resolution. You get better results throwing away pixels than having to make them.

Cleaning Up and Repairing Old Photos

The Clone tool (represented by the rubber stamp icon) can be used to put the head of your son or daughter on the family dog and vice versa. Or, in a less dramatic way, it can be used to clean up and repair old family photos. You can remove dirt spots and stains and patch the picture where the emulsion has cracked.

There are two schools of thought about using the Clone tool. With the first method, the cloning or cleaning is on the background layer (see pages 25–28 for using layers). This alters the picture file, because it changes pixels. The second way is to create a new layer and do all your cloning on that new layer. The advantage of using layers is that you can turn them on or off, and you can completely reverse everything you did by turning off the layer or discarding it. The disadvantage is that layers increase file size.

I have used both methods. I am not so worried about reversibility, because I always **work on a duplicate**. So, I can always go back to my untouched original, make another duplicate, and redo the process. However, file size can be an issue if you have a large, high-resolution file and an old computer; it can make everything go very slowly. Use the method that works for you.

Before you start work on the scanned file, create a duplicate of it, and work on the copy. Use the Zoom tool (its icon is a magnifying glass) to move in on the picture to at least 50%. Here, we have zoomed in to 100%.

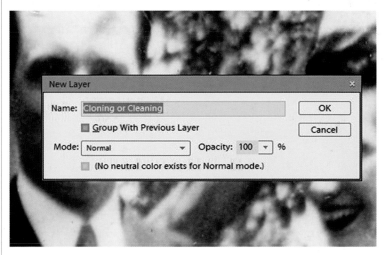

Create a new layer on which you will do your cloning or cleaning (*Layer > New > Layer*). When the New Layer dialog box comes up, you will have the opportunity to name the layer.

Click on the Clone tool. When you are using a separate layer, as we are for cloning, make sure the check boxes in the Options menu for Aligned and All Layers are checked. For this photo, we zoomed in 200% to make it easier to see as we cleaned up a large white spot next to Emmette's head.

This portion of the picture was cleaned using the Clone tool on a new layer. Using a series of Clone stamps, we cleaned up scratches, spots, and other distracting dirt from the old print that we scanned.

From the drop-down menu, we selected a 17-pixel brush that is just a little larger than the spot. Note that we used a soft-edge brush so our stamps would blend into the image. We then selected an area just below the white spot by using Alt-click (PC) or Option-click (Mac) for stamping over the white spot. Using only one click or stamp on top of the white spot did not completely cover it.

The eyeball to the left of the cleaned-up layer is turned off to see what the original photo looked like.

A lot of work goes into restoring old photos, so remember to save them as Master files (page 23).

Using the same selection areas around the white spot, we covered it with three or four stamps. In this way, they blended in so the cloning would not be obvious.

THE FIVE RIGHTS OF USING THE CLONE TOOL

1. Be on the Right Layer. Make sure you are on either the background layer or the special Cloning/Cleaning layer you created.

2. Use the Right Brush. The Clone tool menu has a wide choice of brush styles; the most useful ones are the soft, round brushes. They come right after the hard, round brushes in the drop-down menu ▼. The hard, round brushes leave a sharp edge around the area that has been cloned, and you can often see that edge in your picture. The soft, round brushes feather out the edges of the area that has been stamped, so you do not see an obvious edge.

3. Clone at the Right Magnification. Use the Zoom tool to enlarge the area of the picture that you want to clean up. I generally clone a picture between 50% and 100% in the viewing window. Although you can move over a picture faster at less magnification, you cannot be as precise.

4. Select the Right Area to Copy. Select an area to copy that is close to the subject that you want to stamp over; you'll be less likely to notice the cloning.

5. Use the Right Amount. If there is a large area that needs to be cleaned up, take small bites of the big spot from several different areas around it. This means that you make a selection and stamp from it, and then select a new source and stamp from that one.

MAKING THE QUILT
Step 1. Printing the Photos

Refer to the Target File Checklist (page 32) to create a Target file for each image. Print each image. Print more fabric than you are going to need for the project, unless you have a specific pattern in mind. After your photos and documents are printed, you are ready to plan the layout of your quilt.

Step 2. Planning the Layout

Peel the printed fabrics from the backing, being careful to avoid stressing the bias as you pull it free. Cut away any large excess fabric as needed. Leave a ½″ seam allowance around your image; this can be trimmed more closely later, depending on which construction methods you choose. Cutting away excess white border fabric allows you to see the arrangements of the elements more clearly.

You may decide to enhance your digital fabric with surface design materials (pages 33–39) before construction. Even with the most beautiful digitally printed fabrics, it can be fun to add extra color or texture. If you plan to fuse, you can iron fusible web to your digital fabrics at this point.

Decide on a background. Below, a commercial print is reminiscent of a bulletin board, but with a bit more texture. Be sure to choose a background that will not dominate your main event digital fabrics too much.

Place the background and then your digital fabric photos on your design wall, and arrange them until they are in a pleasing composition. Are the elements too even, too structured? Are they too unbalanced? Refer to Design Basics (pages 42–47) for guidance. Be sure to check your composition as you work (see Secret, page 48).

Arrange your digital photos on the background fabric.

Step 3. Adding Other Fabric Elements

If you plan to add another element, such as the hands in our quilt, you can either use digitally printed photographs on fabrics or try Lura's inked techniques working from photos. For details on drawing and shading techniques, see pages 36–37 and page 77.

USING A PRINTED IMAGE

Pose the hands, and take a photograph of them in the position you want. Watch your light source, and make sure that the shadows will not overpower the image. A soft, diffused light source works well and prevents harsh shadows. You might try other ideas when posing the hands, such as a hand holding the edge of a photo or card or a pen. There are many possibilities. If you wish, you can work with these images in Photoshop Elements and produce them as digital photo fabric, like the rest of the project.

TRACING, INKING, AND SHADING FROM YOUR PHOTOGRAPH

Another option is to draw and ink the hands, as shown, adding an original art look to your project.

Print the hand photos on paper. Place a write-on transparency film sheet over the photo. Trace the outlines of the hands onto the transparency with an ultra-fine Sharpie marker.

Place the traced transparency onto a lightbox, or tape it to a bright window. For inking fabrics, you will need to Dot Test (page 36) them to make sure the fabric won't bleed. Unbleached muslins are usually good; however, starting with a skin-toned fabric lends some extra punch. Lura chose a commercial print that also had some texture.

If desired, press the fabric to freezer paper to stabilize it. Start by using a Prismacolor pencil in a color similar to the color you will use for the inking and shading, and trace the lines onto your fabric.

Refer to Punch It Up (pages 33–39) and Make Your Mark (pages 75–79) for inking and shading techniques. When shading the hands, be sure to strip away plenty of ink on your rub cloth from the Fantastix applicators so you can add soft tones, gradually building them up. Refer to your

photo to see where the shading lies. When you are satisfied with your shading, cut away the excess, leaving ½"
seam allowances. If fusing, iron the fusible to the hands
before trimming.

Tracing a photo onto fabric, then inking and shading it, adds another
element and a different look to your project.

Add the hands to your quilt top. Each new element
added to your design requires a new appraisal. Move the
elements around until you are satisfied. Check your project
in a mirror or with a reducing lens. Are the hands strong
enough in value to read clearly against the other elements?
Perhaps you need to add more tone and shading to make
them strong enough. You might also decide to enhance
your original photos now that the project is beginning
to come together. Always consider the whole surface. If
you plan to use a border, add that to your design wall.
Again, you may decide something needs to be enhanced
or changed.

To add depth, Lura inked a drop shadow behind the left and lower
edges of each element: photos, postcards, and hands. Then, she inked
pins into the tops of the photos and postcards to enhance the effect
of a real bulletin board.

Step 4. Finishing

Once you have all the elements arranged to your liking,
you are ready to put your quilt together. Whether you
use hand or machine appliqué, fusing, piecing, or a combination (pages 48–51) will depend on the project and
your favorite techniques. In this case, fusing and machine
appliqué were used.

Quilting is the final element of design, to add line, color,
and texture. Whether it is done by hand or machine, you
have many options. Quilt as desired, bind, add a sleeve
for hanging, and attach a label.

use color sliders and repeating images

JaneAnn's Dow, 40″ × 41″, by Lura Schwarz Smith, 2008.

CHANGING REAL TO SURREAL FOR DAZZLING COLOR

Starting with a realistic image, vary the color from real to surreal in multiple images for an art quilt that pops with color. Choose an image you like, and try repeating it in a variety of colors. Repeats can be combined in an organized and structured way, or they can be used in a more free-form manner.

As a lifelong rockhound, Lura has picked up, dug up, hunted for, hauled, and even purchased more rocks and minerals than we can count. The house is filled with them. For many rockhounds, crystalline forms are the royalty of the mineral kingdom. Natural quartz crystals are clear, but once Lura started playing with the color sliders in Elements, it became obvious that coloring a clear quartz crystal was going to be too much fun to pass up. This is how we explored multiple color and repeat images.

It seems that rockhounds have a way of discovering each other. JaneAnn Dow was a student in one of Lura's classes in Maui. JaneAnn was a very special person: a teacher, counselor, and healer. To honor her work with the terminally ill, particularly with children, we started with a photo Kerby took of one of JaneAnn's favorite crystals. We printed it once in real color at 11″ × 17″, and then in a series of multicolored image repeats, all at 8½″ × 11″.

The original Dow crystal that Kerby photographed at JaneAnn's home in Maui is a clear white color.

MATERIALS

NOTE: This project offers guidelines and techniques for creating your own unique photo project rather than specifics for an exact replica of our project. Select materials as appropriate for your project.

Digital images that will work well for color changes

Prepared fabric sheets

Silks or satins for areas of emphasis

Fabric for backing

Fabric for binding or optional facing

Batting

OPTIONAL FOR FREE-FORM PIECING:
Rotary cutter and mat

QUICK COLOR CHANGES

Open a Master file (page 23) of the image for which you want to change the color. Make a duplicate, and close the Original file. The Quick Edit mode of Photoshop Elements allows you to make quick and easy color changes to a picture. The Before and After views show you right away the changes you are making to your image.

This method changes all the color in the whole picture. If you don't like the changes you made, click the Reset button at the top of the After view to change the image back to the original and start all over.

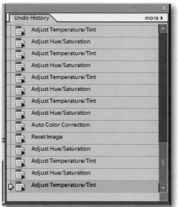

When you return to Full Edit, notice that any color changes are listed in the Undo History palette. The last change made is always at the bottom of the list. You still have an opportunity to undo your color change here by stepping back or clicking up in your history of changes.

Slide to Taste: There are four sliders in the Color palette: Saturation, Hue, Temperature, and Tint. Slide them left or right to change the color. Once you have changed the color, click on the green check box to save the change.

Now you are ready to save your image as a new Master file. Once you have saved it, close it, and open your first Master with the original color. Repeat the process, using the color sliders to create another image in a different color.

This is the Master file of the crystal in the blue-purple color range.

Repeat the process, starting with a duplicate of the Master file in the original color. Here we shifted the color of the crystal to green and orange.

MAKING THE QUILT

Step 1. Printing the Photos

Refer to Process Your Pictures for Printing on Fabric (pages 17–32) to create your Target files. Print the images. Print more fabric than you are going to need for the project, unless you have a specific pattern in mind. After your photos are printed, you are ready to plan the composition of your quilt.

Step 2. Planning and Composition

Arrange the printed images on your design wall, and begin to add other fabrics. As you work with your images, consider the construction style that will best suit your project. What shapes are your digital images? You can enhance this imagery by the way you construct your quilt. If there are mostly straight-edged forms in your photo, such as buildings, you might choose a straight-line construction and a more structured composition. Curved forms might work well with a curved treatment to echo and emphasize these shapes.

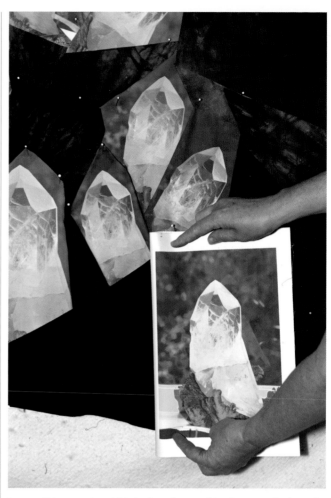

Lura auditions a printed fabric sheet for possible placement in the quilt top. To contrast with the color spectrum of the printed crystals, richly toned dark fabrics help lend a glow. Quartz crystals are found underground, so the darker fabrics give the feeling of a cavelike atmosphere. For a hint of the glitter of different ores, a few silk and satin fabrics are included.

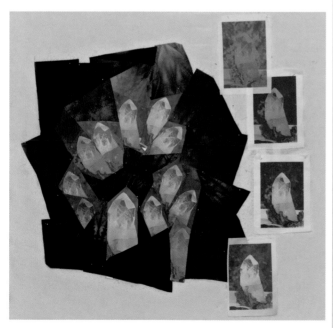

After the digitally colored crystals were printed, Lura placed them on the design wall and began to bring in other fabrics. Because crystals are a natural form, she wanted to give the project an organic look, with loose groupings and odd angles that harmonized with the facets of the crystals, rather than using a more organized pattern.

Step 3. Construction

Cut all the fabrics a little oversized, using free cuts (no ruler) with a rotary cutter. The excess gives leeway for later adjustments in the composition, as well as for overlaps that will be needed in the piecing process. For this project, using a ruler for a mechanical, perfectly straight cut would be distracting, so even the fairly straight cuts were done freehand.

Putting it all together is like figuring out a puzzle—a fun challenge when there are many pieces.

When the composition comes together, the construction can begin. Free-form piecing (pages 49–51) works well for this project.

Step 4. Finishing Free-Form Quilts without a Binding

To let the image flow right off the edge and to allow for free-form edges, use a facing rather than a binding. If your quilt top is small, you can use another whole piece of equal-size fabric to make a simple pillowcase turn: Make a sandwich by layering first the batting and then the quilt top, both right side **up**; then add the backing fabric, right side **down,** so the right sides of the top and the backing are together. Pin and stitch the edges, leaving a small area to turn your project right side out. Clip the corners and any deep curves or angles as needed; then turn. Using a blunt knitting needle or chopstick, carefully but fully push out corners and any angles. Press, invisibly hand stitch the opening, baste, and quilt.

For a more sizeable piece, create a facing. Choose a backing for the quilt, and then layer and quilt as usual, leaving some excess for trim at the edges. After the quilting is complete, trim carefully, leaving a ¼" seam allowance at the edges. Cut 2"-wide facing fabric strips for each side of the quilt, adding 4" extra length. Place right sides together, leaving a 2" overhang at each end. Pin and stitch the facings to the front of the quilt on opposite sides, right sides together. Clip any deep curves or angles carefully. Turn the facings to the back side, making sure the seam turns completely so the facings do not show on the front. Repeat on the remaining two sides. Trim any excess fabric at the corners. Fold to miter on the back side, adjusting if the corners are free cut and not square. Hand stitch the facing to the back of the quilt.

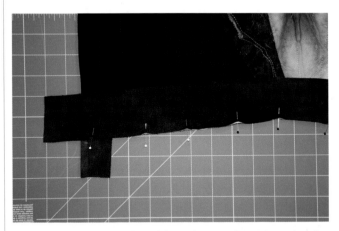

To allow the fabrics and colors of the quilt top to flow right to the edge of the quilt, and to accommodate free-form edges, a facing provides a good finishing option in place of a binding.

capture a collage

Wild Kitty, 33″ × 46″, by Kerby C. Smith, 2008.

MULTIPLE IMAGES TELL THE STORY

Some ideas start with a single photo. We were teaching on Maui in Hawaii and staying Up Country at a friend's home. She had an old house cat that had adopted a younger feral tiger cat. One day, we saw the small buff-gray tiger come slinking out of the brush at the edge of the backyard. Kerby was amazed at how the striped cat blended into the landscape so you almost didn't see him. The standoffish cat was simply called Wild Kitty. In the afternoons, we would sit out back and watch this young cat perform his appearing and disappearing act at mealtime. It all started with one photo, and then of course, Kerby took a few more.

When we got home, Kerby printed out fabric sheets of Wild Kitty in various sizes and suggested to Lura that there was a quilt idea in the images. He even pinned them up on her secondary design wall to inspire her. But she didn't see the wonderful possibilities of this camouflaged critter: the dull grays and browns didn't grab her attention. So Kerby took on this quilt project himself.

Kerby's vision of *Wild Kitty* was a free-form art quilt—no traditional quilt blocks here. The design evolved from the mixing of digitally printed photos on fabric with commercial and hand-dyed fabric raided from Lura's stash. Kerby also learned a very important lesson: Always ask permission before using fabric from someone else's stash, even if you live in a community property state.

MATERIALS

NOTE: This project offers guidelines and techniques for creating your own unique photo project rather than specifics for an exact replica of our project. Select materials as appropriate for your project.

Multiple digital images of one subject

Prepared fabric sheets

Background fabric for base, 3″ larger on all sides than the intended project top

Additional fabrics to blend and contrast with digital fabrics

Fusible web or spray adhesives, such as Sulky KK 2000 or 505 Spray and Fix

Fabric for backing and binding

Batting

Stretcher bars

MAKING THE QUILT

Step 1. Printing the Photos

Refer to Process Your Pictures for Printing on Fabric (pages 17–32) to create your Target files. Print the images. Print more fabric than you are going to need for the project, unless you have a specific pattern in mind. After your photos are printed, you are ready to begin.

Step 2. Looking at Your Imagery

Place all your printed fabric images on the design wall.

Putting all your digital fabric images on your design wall allows you to see all the options you have to work with in creating your quilt top.

Step 3. Beginning a Collage with a Base Fabric

After you have your basic set of working images, bring in other fabrics that will go well with the color palette of your pictures. Look for one piece of fabric that you can use as a background for your art quilt. Cut the piece of fabric a little larger than you want the quilt to be. This fabric will be the canvas for your quilt on the design wall.

Find a fabric background.

Step 4. Playing with the Fabric

Start playing with fabric—cutting it and pinning it to your fabric background until you are pleased with the design. You might find that you have too many images on your canvas. Sometimes less is more.

Although this is a free-form process, all the elements of a collage need to be carefully considered. Taking away fabric in this collage resulted in a strong design statement.

Step 5. Fusing or Using Spray Adhesives

It's time to turn your design into a quilt top. Having been influenced by Laura Wasilowski and her fusing methods, Kerby decided that this quilt top would be completely fused. However, he did not like using fusible web and release paper. Instead, he wanted the freedom of pasting down the fabric, as if he were creating a paper collage. Kerby attached the printed fabrics to the background using a temporary spray adhesive.

> NOTE: Sulky KK 2000 is nonflammable, whereas 505 is extremely flammable (according to the information on the cans). Use in very well-ventilated areas or outside in the fresh air.

Kerby refined his design and then used fabric spray adhesive to attach the fabric pieces to the background material.

Step 6. Stitching and Constructing the Top

After you have fused or glued your fabric to your background, it's time to stitch it down to create your quilt top. For this project, nylon thread was used as the top thread to make the stitching of the top disappear. This enhanced the collage look of mixing the digital fabrics with the other fabrics.

Step 7. Quilting the Project

When it came time to make the quilt, Kerby chose a low-loft batt. He took the responsible attitude and learned to machine quilt his project. *Wild Kitty* uses a variety of top threads—but note the use of black thread. To make the cat faces pop, black top thread was used to emphasize the cat's mouth.

Step 8. Finishing with Stretcher Bars

Because Kerby was already accustomed to stretching his photo art canvases, he chose to do the same with *Wild Kitty* after it was quilted. He wrapped the quilt to the back of wooden stretcher bars and stapled the edges.

Simple Pleasures, 7" × 10", by Kerby C. Smith, 2006.

Kerby first experimented with canvas and fabric collage on a donation piece for Hurricane Katrina victims. He combined scanned bluejay feathers and photos in *Simple Pleasures*. Digital images on photo canvas are extremely vivid and rich because of the ink receptor coatings on the sealed canvas surface.

Collaged art quilt postcards have all three layers of a traditional quilt. The tops of these postcards were printed on canvas and stitched together. The middle layer is fusible on both sides to hold the top and back together before stitching down the edges. The back of the quilt is digitally printed fabric. These postcards are from a series combining Kerby's photos of our roses and Chihuly glass.

Protect, Save, Enjoy, 18″ × 33″, by Georgia B. Heller, 2008.

PHOTO BY C&T PUBLISHING

Double Take, 23″ × 22″, by Lura Schwarz Smith, 2008.

Combining the vivid cat images printed on canvas with other fabrics, this is Lura's small version of *Wild Kitty*.

PHOTO BY C&T PUBLISHING

Winter, 21″ × 13″, by Diana Roberts, 2007.

layer on the effects and colors

Buster's Blues, 36″ × 39″, by Lura Schwarz Smith, 2009.

USING LAYERS FOR SPECIAL EFFECTS

Buster is our Chocolate Labrador Retriever. He loves to go for morning walks, and he pines if he doesn't get to go each day. Kerby had been working on a series of "Walking the Dog" photographs, but no single image seemed to convey Buster's blues when he did not get to go for his daily walk.

In *Buster's Blues*, image repeats, color replacement, and size variations add movement and energy to the composition.

MATERIALS

NOTE: This project offers guidelines and techniques for creating your own unique photo project rather than specifics for an exact replica of our project. Select materials as appropriate for your project.

Digital images that will work well for color replacements

Prepared fabric sheets

Additional fabrics that work with the images

Fabrics for backing and binding

Batting

OPTIONAL FOR ENHANCING DIGITAL FABRICS:

Surface design materials (pages 33–39)

LAYERS AND CHANGING COLOR

Layers are one of the most powerful aspects of Photoshop Elements. They have many uses, from making basic adjustments to creating interesting effects. For *Buster's Blues*, a duplicate was created (page 20), and the Clone tool (pages 55–57) was used to remove unwanted items from the photo.

Portrait of Buster waiting to go for a walk.

The Clone tool was used to remove the foot and bench in the upper right corner of the picture.

Creating Composite Images with Layers

One of the best things about Photoshop is that you can easily create a composite image using Layers.

> ▸▸ Secret
>
> To use Layers, you need to be in Full Edit.

To create a composite image, open in Full Edit (*File > Open*) the two Master picture files that you want to use. After making duplicates (page 20), check to make sure that both pictures are in the same color space (page 14) and at the same resolution (page 7). If one picture is at 300 ppi and the other at 180 ppi, the picture at the lower resolution will be smaller when they are combined.

Both pictures of Buster were 8-bit and 360 ppi. The picture of him running was intentionally sized smaller. The larger, main picture is the Master file portrait of Buster. The image of him running was set into the portrait.

The picture that you want to place on top of the other picture should be the active window. I like to move the active picture off the main picture using the Move tool (the top icon in the toolbar), so I can see where I am dragging. From the Layers palette bin, drag the Background layer of the active picture onto the larger, receiving picture. Once you finish the drag, the active window will switch to the receiving picture, and you will see Layer 1 above the Background layer in the Layers palette bin.

▶▶ Secret

Always drag a Background layer from the Layers palette. Do not attempt to drag a picture from the Project bin at the bottom of the screen. The thumbnail images in the Project bin are not the right size for dropping into another picture.

Here is the portrait of Buster and a picture of him running. The running picture is the one we want to drop into the portrait of Buster. Note that the picture of Buster running is the active window. Move it off the portrait so you can see where you are dragging its Background layer.

Once you have dragged a Background layer onto your main image, you can use the Move tool to position the top picture. Here the running dog picture has been placed to the right of Buster's portrait.

Click on the Eraser tool. Then select a large soft brush from the options bar to erase the square edges of the running dog picture until it blends into the main picture. Use short moves with the Eraser tool so you can back up in your history in case you erase too much of the picture in the new layer.

Replacing Color to Get a Blue Buster

To increase the feeling of the blue funk that Buster is in because he is not out on his daily walk, his brown coat was made blue. To change the color, first create a duplicate layer to work on (*Layer > Duplicate Layer*), and relabel it Color Change.

Click the Foreground Color box at the bottom of the toolbar. The eyedropper icon appears, and the Select Foreground Color dialog box appears. Move the cursor and the vertical slider to select a color.

The Color Replacement tool (selected from the drop-down menu on the Paintbrush tool) can now be used to replace Buster's brown coat with blue. Select a soft brush from the *Options* menu, and use short moves to change his color.

When you are done, save this new file as a Master. In the naming protocol (page 31), use an L to indicate that it is a Master file with layers. For example, this file is named Blue Buster ML.tif.

The background was cropped away (page 30), and the picture was flipped (*Image > Rotate > Flip Horizontal*) for the final portrait of a blue Buster.

MAKING THE QUILT

NOTE: These are examples; steps will vary for each project.

Step 1. Printing the Photos

Refer to Process Your Pictures for Printing on Fabric (pages 17–32) to create your Target files. Print the images. Print more fabric than you are going to need for the project, unless you have a specific pattern in mind. After your photos and documents are printed, you are ready to design the layout of your quilt.

Step 2. Designing the Layout

Place the digital fabrics on your design wall, and begin to bring in other fabrics. The repeats and reversals of images are a good challenge and offer the opportunity to add a sense of rhythm to the composition. In general, closer images are larger and lower in the composition; the more distant, smaller images are higher. For example, the running figure of Buster graduates from smaller and farther up in the composition, to larger and lower in the composition. The head shots of Buster also move from small in the distance to large up close.

Step 3. Adding Other Fabrics

As the composition comes together, add other fabrics, working with the basic colors of the digital photo fabrics. In this case, the blues, greens, and buff colors of the added fabrics echo the digital prints. Echoing existing shapes can also be a useful technique in your design. The cast shadows of Kerby and Buster are completed and elongated at the base by adding a gradated gray fabric cut out to complete the forms. To the right, two overlapping shadows of Kerby are printed on silk chiffon and fused to echo the overlapping airy look of the other digital prints.

Step 4. Enhancing the Images

Sometimes digital fabrics can use a little boost from surface design materials (pages 33–39).

The blue theme is echoed with blue highlights on the brown dog head and along the shadows. These highlights were added using water-soluble oil pastels without water.

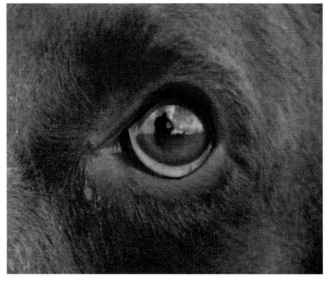

Buster's close-up has a wonderful tiny reflection of Kerby's silhouette in each eye. Fabrico markers were used to enhance that detail, and the nose and other details were punched up with oil pastels, inks, markers, and Prismacolor pencils.

Step 5. Construction, Quilting, and Finishing

Construct your quilt top according on your project and how you like to work. In this case, machine piecing and quilting were used. Machine or hand quilt, bind, and add the sleeve and label.

Buster's Blues
All Rights Reserved by
Lura Schwarz Smith, 2009
P.O. Box 649, Coarsegold, CA 93614
www.lura-art.com
Photos by Kerby C. Smith

make your mark

Imagine, 23" × 19", by Lura Schwarz Smith, 2007.

The two left portraits of John Lennon in *Imagine* are digital photo fabrics.
The right one was traced with a blue Fabrico marker and shaded with purple
Tsukineko ink to produce the hand-done face to the right.

ADDING DRAWING AND SHADING ON FABRIC

Why go to all the effort to create hand-drawn and shaded images on fabric when you can just print out beautiful digital photographs? For one thing, it results in quite a different effect. Why does any artist bother to draw and paint when there are cameras around? Photography is one art form, and drawing is another, and the combination of the two can give your project a very personal, individual look. Many people believe they cannot draw realistically, but using Lura's easy tracing and simple shading system, you can combine drawing and shading with your digital images to lend a wonderful individuality to your project. Lura has successfully taught this technique to hundreds of students, so jump in and give it a try.

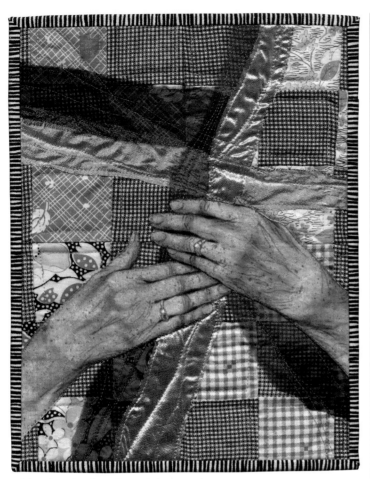

Golden Thread, 8½″ × 11″, Lura Schwarz Smith, 2004.

Golden Thread is the result of traced, inked, and shaded hands fused over pieced and fused fabrics.

Winter Vineyard, 29″ × 18″, by Lura Schwarz Smith, 2006.

Various techniques are used in *Winter Vineyard*: direct drawing on fabric with inks and markers, a photographic digital print on fabric, and Lura's watercolor vignette scanned and digitally printed.

MATERIALS

NOTE: This project offers guidelines and techniques for creating your own unique photo project rather than specifics for an exact replica of our project. Select materials as appropriate for your project.

Nonbleed fabrics for inking (page 36)

Paper

Prismacolor Artists Colored Pencils

Transparency film sheets

Sharpie Ultra-Fine marker

White plastic art eraser (comes on many mechanical pencils)

Tsukineko All Purpose Inks and Fantastix applicators

Lightbox or window for tracing

Freezer paper, if desired for stabilizing fabric

Blue painter's tape

▶▶ Secret

To further explore the delights of drawing and shading, check the recommended reading list under Resources (page 94). Get a sketchbook—and use it! We are constantly surrounded by drawing opportunities.

BASIC SHADING

Begin practicing on paper with Prismacolor pencils. There are many good brands of colored pencils, but this brand works particularly well on both fabrics and paper. Applying inks to fabrics in the dry brush method will be quite similar to using colored pencils on paper.

Smooth Gradients of Tone

Make a series of boxes at least 1″ × 1″. With a colored pencil, press firmly to get deep, rich color; then gradually use less pressure to get lighter tones. Practice getting a smooth gradation from the darkest (harder pressure) to lightest possible tone and—this is the tricky part—leaving some of the white of the paper still showing in each box. This takes great strength of character, as our inclination is to fill in a shape completely, just like we once did in coloring books. Repeat this exercise until you get smooth, nonstriped gradients that fade away to the white of your paper inside each box. This uncolored area is the all-important highlights area.

Gradient tones should be smooth. Leave some white paper showing for a highlight, as with watercolors.

Light Sources

Determining your light source is a vital part of the shading process. Study light and shadow in photos, art, and everyday life all around you. Where is the light source? Outside, the sun is a single light source. A room with multiple lights across the ceiling and with outdoor light streaming in side windows is a complex lighting system. In the sample shading exercise (page 78), the arrows show a single light source that makes shading easier. These shapes will give you an alphabet of simple forms to begin to understand how light and shadow work.

Light and Shadow

The basics of light and shadow are:

Highlight: Where light falls directly on the object

Midtones: The area between highlight and shadow on the object

Shadow: Deepening shade on the part of the object away from the light source

Reflected Light: Less bright than highlight; a glow that bounces back on the object

Cast Shadow: The shadow cast by the object onto a background or other object

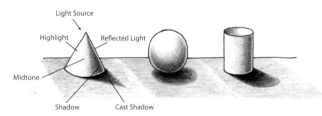

Light and shadow are demonstrated very simply on these three basic shapes.

Draw the three simple shapes, and copy the shading. Note that you can use your pencil strokes to help define the shape of the form (curved lines that follow the curve of the object or straight strokes for a flat surface). Find examples of the bounce of reflected light in your surroundings. Place an egg on a brightly colored surface under a bright light, and note that not only light but also color bounce back onto an object. See how cast shadows are darkest close to the source, then diffuse and lighten the farther away the shadow falls. Notice the elegant subtleties in the way light and shadows give our world dimension. Begin to see more!

SUCCESSFUL TRACING

This is the original photo of Lura's mother's hands used in *Golden Thread*.

A clear, good-quality photograph works best for tracing. Working with an image at least 5″ in size will help you get details and to trace and shade it well. If your photo is very small, scan it at a good resolution (page 6), and print it larger without losing definition. An 8½″ × 11″ photo is a good size to print out.

Many photographs have complex or multiple light sources. This is often the case when a flash is used, as the ambient sunlight or room light may come from a different angle. Begin with a fairly simple photo with an obvious light source. A single light source provides a more obvious play of light and shadow. If your project has an unclear or complex light source, choose just one light source, and shade it accordingly.

Place a write-on transparency sheet over your photo. Use a bit of painter's tape to hold the transparency in position. Using the Sharpie marker, carefully trace the image onto the transparency. Trace all the information you will need, but not so much that the lines are overwhelming. What are the most important lines of your image? Some lines that are important but less defined (like a smile crease or a color change on a flower petal) can be indicated with a broken line. This dotted line will be your cue to trace a softer, lighter line with your Prismacolor pencil when you work on the fabric. Slide a piece of plain white paper under the transparency to check your tracing and to be sure that you have not missed any lines. If any lines need to be redone, use the white plastic art eraser to remove the Sharpie line from the transparency.

If the main shading will be done with Tsukineko inks, choose a fabric that is as light as the highlight you want. Leave highlight areas untoned, and add the rest of the shading and color.

Place the transparency on a lightbox or tape it to a window. If desired, press your fabric to freezer paper for stability in tracing. Use tape to stabilize the fabric over the transparency. Using a Prismacolor pencil, carefully trace the image onto your fabric. Choose a color that is not too pale, or it will disappear immediately when you begin to add shading with the inks.

NOTE: Remember, when you see the dotted lines on the transparency, this is your cue for a softer line—trace a solid line more lightly with the Prismacolor pencil. Dots are harder to "disappear" into the shading.

Check your fabric tracing by turning off the lightbox and viewing the tracing carefully. Have you missed any lines? Can you see the colored pencil lines clearly? Be sure you have all the details you need.

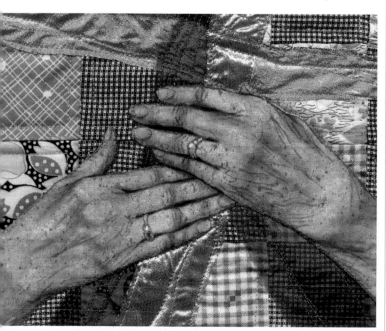

Inking on a textured, skin-tone fabric adds realism to the hands in this detail of *Golden Thread*.

INKING AND SHADING YOUR PROJECT

First practice the dry brush inking techniques (page 37) before you start coloring your project. For shading delicate, blended tones, be sure you have rubbed off enough ink from the pointed brush tip Fantastix. Start with the more shadowed areas, and build your tones gradually. Remember to leave highlight areas uncolored to let the light of the fabric show—you can always tone this down later by adding more ink, but you cannot take it out once applied.

Adding Emphasis

Textile markers give an intense application of ink and will add line and detail for emphasis. For small areas, Prismacolor pencils can be used for shading. The other materials covered on pages 34–39 can also be considered. Compare your own version with the photographic source as you work, paying special attention to values. Have you shaded enough?

New techniques take practice. Doing several versions is a great way to learn. Save each version, and then view them together on your design wall—right side up, upside down, in a mirror. Determine just what you like and do not about each one. This will make each effort valuable. Even with an attempt that isn't your favorite, you might find a part of the shading and drawing that is more successful than in another version, and you can use this information to ultimately make a project you are completely happy with.

Go back to the quilts at the beginning of this chapter, and take a good look to see how drawing and shading were incorporated into each quilt.

stir it up

Gary's Twirl, 18" × 18", by Lura Schwarz Smith, 2008.

MATERIALS

NOTE: This project offers guidelines and techniques for creating your own unique photo project rather than specifics for an exact replica of our project. Select materials as appropriate for your project.

Digitally printed photo fabrics using filters and effects

Other fabrics that work with the digital fabric

Fabrics for backing and binding

Batting

OPTIONAL FOR ENHANCING DIGITAL FABRICS:
Surface design materials (pages 33–39)

USING FILTERS TO GO FROM ORDINARY TO ABSTRACT

Use filters in Photoshop Elements to twist, twirl, flip, and manipulate your image to create new and abstracted imagery in your quilts.

Our son, Gary, has become interested in photography, and he always seems to find an unusual point of view through his camera lens. He took this slightly soft close-up of a battered old water nozzle, and let us use the image to experiment with various filters and effects, including color sliders, to morph the original image.

PHOTO BY GARY SMITH

Original image of a water nozzle used for *Gary's Twirl*.

FUN WITH FILTERS

Traditionally, photographers have developed their images secluded in darkrooms and surrounded by mysterious chemicals. In creating Photoshop, Adobe has brought image developing out of the dark. It has filled the photographic process with light and made it easy for everyone to let his or her imagination soar.

Photoshop Elements includes a giant amusement park called Filter (available in either Full Edit or Quick Edit). This is where Lura went to play with the water nozzle photo.

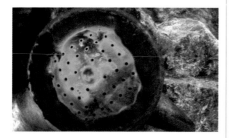

Selecting *Filter > Stylize > Solarize* produced a solarization of the water nozzle picture.

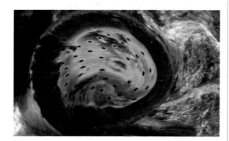

Selecting *Filter > Distort > Twirl* spun the water nozzle image to abstraction.

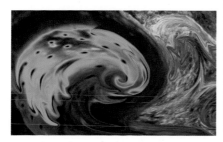

Selecting *Filter > Distort > Liquefy* provided another whole set of tools for pushing color around the image.

Next, Lura created her Master file (page 23) before using the Color sliders to create different-colored Target files (page 29).

FROM COMPUTER SCREEN TO FABRIC

Lura's abstract images looked great on screen, but they turned out very flat on her fabric test print (page 27). This is the phenomenon we mentioned earlier—images projected on screen look brighter than those printed.

If you experience the same thing, refer to pages 26–27 to create adjustment layers for Brightness/Contrast, Levels, and Hue/Saturation. Remember, the Layer menu is only available in Full Edit.

Another way to make an overall adjustment to the image is to use a Levels Adjustment Layer (page 26). Check the Preview box so you can see the changes in the main window. Although the dialog box includes an Auto button, the changes it makes are often a bit too radical. Above the Auto button is the Reset button, which you can click to go back to the unchanged original; you can then use the sliders to adjust the image manually nstead.

Making adjustments on screen may look too bright and have too much contrast. The real determination will be the fabric you are using and the type of inks in your printer. You may need to make several test prints to get it right.

Adding text to pictures is easy. First choose *Image > Resize > Canvas Size* (see page 27) to add some canvas around your image so you have a place for a line of text. Next, turn on the rulers around the picture (*View > Rulers*), as this is helpful when placing text. **Note:** The rulers only appear on screen; they will not appear when you print your picture.

Click on the Text tool and select font, style, size, and alignment from the *Text* menu. Wherever you click with the Text cursor is where your line of text will start; this also automatically creates a Text layer.

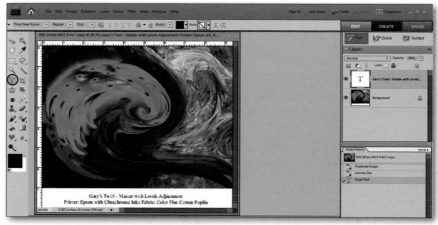

Choosing the Text Tool allows you to add a line of text to your sample print.

MIRROR IMAGES

The final step that Lura performed to get all the fabric she wanted was to create a set of files that were the reverse of the originals. To do so, she selected *Image > Rotate > Flip Layer Horizontal.* She then created her Master files.

After making a duplicate of your original Master file, it is easy to create a mirror image of it. Flipping the layer horizontally (*Image > Rotate > Flip Layer Horizontal*) gave us a mirror image of the original.

MAKING THE QUILT

Step 1. Printing the Photos

Refer to Process Your Pictures for Printing on Fabric (pages 17–32) to create your Target files. Print the images. Print more fabric than you are going to need for the project, unless you have a specific pattern in mind. After your photos and documents are printed, you are ready to begin the design process.

Step 2. Designing with Abstract Images

Peel the printed fabrics from the backing, being careful to avoid stressing the bias as you pull them free. The pairs, with the reversals, lend themselves to an informal mirrored treatment.

Integrating digital fabrics with others in your stash is always a fun challenge. When using filters, sometimes the image is changed so much it is unrecognizable from the original. For example, Gary was unable to tell which photo of his was the starting point. In working with highly abstracted photographs like this, it can be very fun to follow the shapes, textures, colors, and moods of the new, changed imagery.

Step 3. Construction

In this case, the swirling shapes seemed to call for a circular construction. The free-form P-free piecing technique (pages 49–51) was used to echo the off-center swirls. Textures in the other fabrics include lively little prints that help spin the eye around the asymmetrical composition.

Step 4. Enhancing the Fabrics

To add a bit more punch, try water-soluble oil pastels (page 39), which give a rich color even used dry. In this quilt, they were used on both the digital fabrics and the other fabrics, helping to integrate them.

Step 5. Quilting and Finishing

To keep the free-form edges without using a binding, we used a pillowcase turn instead. To do so, make a sandwich by layering the batting and then the top, both right side up. Then add the backing so right sides are together with the top. Machine stitch along the edges, leaving a small space for turning. Clip the corners and turn. A blunt knitting needle or small artist's paintbrush handle can be used to carefully turn and extend seams and corners fully. Press the edges, being sure that the backing does not show at the front of the piece. Hand stitch the opening closed, and then machine or hand quilt. In this case, machine quilting echoes the swirling forms. Finally, add a sleeve and a label.

REALISM FROM ABSTRACT DIGITAL FABRIC

Sometimes the imagery in digital fabrics can be abstract, even if the quilt's subject matter is not. In one of our classes, Sonja Campbell manipulated her images in a very different way for a special effect. She used photos of both people and architecture from her trip to India and condensed them into narrow segments of digital fabrics. Six different digital fabrics were made from different photos. In the digital fabric she created, highly compressed images formed patterns rather than images. Folding this fabric into narrow pleats to form the garments of her figures further distorted and abstracted these images.

Russian Lady, 32″ × 53″, by Sonja Campbell, 2008.

PHOTO BY GARY CAMPBELL

Radha and Krishna, 31″ × 45″, by Sonja Campbell, 2007.

Sonja Campbell's images are condensed and printed on digital fabrics.

After a trip to Russia with her husband, Sonja used a photo of a Soviet-era mosaic at the space center, greatly enlarged, for the background fabric. She abstracted and created digital fabrics from other Russian photos for the woman's costume, which were then embellished with tulle and beading. This produces a lovely image that is imbued with layers of meaning and memory from their trip.

fractured mirror

Shadowplay, 33″ × 26″, by Lura Schwarz Smith, 2007.

MAKING A MULTIPLE VIEW

Use different views of the same image to create a multi-dimensional look. You don't have to be a Picasso to use more than one point of view at once.

By photographing an object or scene from different angles, you can fracture, repeat, and give new dimension to what was once a realistic image. Using other fabrics and adding surface design elements can all contribute to an interesting, more abstracted scene.

As a professional photographer, Kerby usually has the latest and greatest DSLR cameras. But Lura likes the small point-and-shoot cameras. One sunny day at the Getty Art Center in Los Angeles, Lura was intrigued by the shadows of the courtyard patio furniture. Armed with her brand-new digital Nikon CoolPix camera, she photographed these shadows from varying angles. We printed multiples of a few of these on 8½" × 11" sheets of pretreated fabric for more options in repeats.

MATERIALS

NOTE: This project offers guidelines and techniques for creating your own unique photo project rather than specifics for an exact replica of our project. Select materials as appropriate for your project.

Digitally printed photo fabrics, 3 or more different views

Other fabrics to blend and contrast

Fabrics for backing and binding

Fusible web (optional if desired for construction)

Batting

OPTIONAL FOR ENHANCING DIGITAL FABRICS:

Surface design materials (pages 33–39)

PHOTO BY LURA SCHWARZ SMITH

Getty: Shadow One

PHOTO BY LURA SCHWARZ SMITH

Getty: Shadow Two

PHOTO BY LURA SCHWARZ SMITH

Getty: Shadow Three

STARTING FROM JPEGS

The files produced by Lura's point-and-shoot camera were JPEGs in the sRGB color space at a resolution of 300 ppi (pages 14, 25, and 26). It is a good habit to sync your image early on in the editing process: After opening and making Duplicates and closing the Originals (pages 19–20), change the images to the correct ppi for your printer (page 7), set the color space to AdobeRGB (page 14), and save the files as TIFFs (page 31).

Changing the color space in Photoshop Elements to AdobeRGB does not add any color to the image. However, it does give you a larger color space to work in if you are doing any of the color manipulations mentioned in other chapters.

The change in resolution does not affect the file size if you link all three document attributes. Make your Master files as needed.

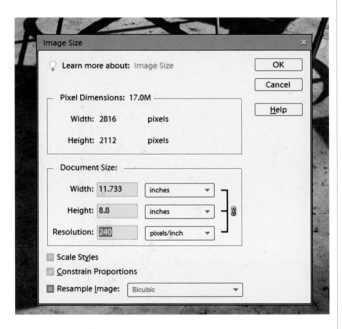

Selecting *Image > Resize > Image Size* brings up the Image Size dialog box. Uncheck Resample Image and there will be a link to the right of the Width, Height, and Resolution document sizes.

MAKING THE QUILT

Step 1. Printing the Photos

Refer to Process Your Pictures for Printing on Fabric (pages 17–32) to create your Target files. Print the images. Print more fabric than you are going to need for the project, unless you have a specific pattern in mind. After your photos and documents are printed, you are ready to design the layout of your quilt.

Step 2. Designing the Layout

Pin your background fabric to the design wall to give unity to the developing project. You may want to audition more than one background fabric, changing them as you work, until you are pleased with your choice.

Step 3. Planning Your Techniques

If you are going to fuse the project, it's easier to apply the fusible web to the digital fabrics before cutting into them. This also enables you to use the entire piece of digital fabric, because fusing allows for intricate and detailed shapes to be easily cut and applied.

Step 4. Using Echo and Repeat in Your Design

View your digital images, and decide which forms and colors you like. Perhaps you can add pieces of other fabrics at this point to echo and extend the shapes in your images. In this project, a repeating tilt was formed by the placement of the rectangular edges of the digital fabrics. The angle of cast shadows was extended into the border with the gray striped fabrics, which echo the slatted effect of the patio furniture shadows.

Step 5. Considering Contrast

These photos of shadows were fairly monochromatic tones of neutrals and grays; so Lura decided to bring in a strong contrast color of red. The large oval shape of a table shadow was echoed in several different sizes and tones of red to move the eye around the composition.

The red element was added with fabrics, art materials, and threads.

Step 6. Enriching and Enhancing the Surface

To add richness to the surface, Lura used water-soluble oil pastels, inks, textile markers, and Prismacolor pencils (pages 33–39) to add enhancements of the muted golds, ochers, whites, and blacks in the fabrics.

Step 7. Bringing It All Together

Lura fused the images to allow precise cutting, overlapping, and placement of the images. A tiny zigzag stitch appliquéd the raw edges in place.

Step 8. Finishing Touches

The border was sewn onto the project, and the final fusing of imagery was allowed to spill out into the border in several places. This breaks up the straight edge of the border and leads the eye into the composition. Machine quilting finished the project, using a contrasting red thread at some places for emphasis.

OTHER WAYS TO USE MULTIPLE IMAGES

Happy Father's Day, 9˝ × 9˝, by Lura Schwarz Smith, 2007.

Multiple printed fabrics add interest, even in a small, simple fabric greeting card. Five different digital prints were combined in this small quilt.

Houses, 30¼˝ × 49¾˝, by Evelyn Taylor, 2008.

Lilikoi Flowers—Passionfruit, 56″ × 57″, by Joan Davis, 2008.

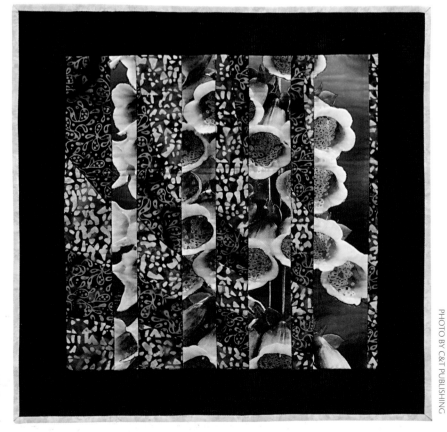

Foxglove, 19″ × 19″, by Marilyn Reinarz, 2008. Quilted by Diana Roberts.

beyond cotton

Stone Dreams, 22" × 41", by Lura Schwarz Smith, 2009.

SILKS, SHEERS, AND TEXTURES

A mix of different fabrics can provide a rich change of physical texture in your work. A little shimmer of silk or a touch of sparkly fabric adds a nice point of interest. For digital printing, prepared fabrics also come in a wide variety. In *Stone Dreams*, Lura made digital prints on silk chiffon, silk organza, and silk charmeuse, as well as on cotton poplin.

To make the face and hand, Lura drew directly on fabrics with a combination of inks, Caran d'Ache pastels, and Prismacolor pencils. If the art effect of drawing is desired as an element, you can use the tracing technique shown on pages 78–79 and work from your own photographs.

Digitally printed textures on sheers are useful in tying together various elements in your project. These silk chiffons were printed with imagery used in *Stone Dreams* and *Buster's Blues (page 70)* and show Lura's hand beneath them.

TEXTURE RUBBINGS FOR FABRICS

In addition to printed textures, extra punch can be added by doing rubbings over textured surfaces. Pentel Fabric Fun Oil Pastel Dye Sticks and Caran d'Ache water-soluble oil pastel crayons were used to create rubbings of rough stone texture to add to the stone texture effect (see pages 38–39).

MERGE THE ELEMENTS WITH SHEER FABRICS

Printing on sheer fabrics is a good way to merge various elements of your design, while also providing continuity with a repeat of imagery or texture. Here, a piece of sheer silk organza printed with stone texture overlays the arm where it seems to emerge from the water. Silk chiffon, which is less sheer than the organza, is used on the figure's shoulder area, and another piece of silk organza overlays the hair at the back of the neck area. Using Misty Fuse is an excellent way to attach sheer fabrics without adding stiffness or opacity.

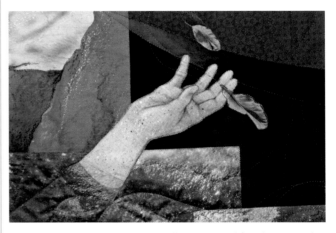

The stone texture printed on sheer silk organza and fused as an overlay blends and merges the fabrics of skin and water.

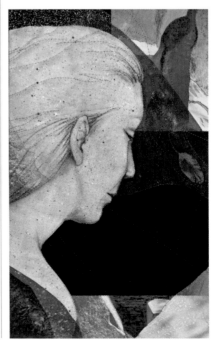

Printed silk chiffon and organza fabrics add depth and texture on the hair and the leaf print behind the head.

Tish B'Av, 8½″ × 11″, by Susan Slesinger, 2006.

Shaded Trail, Secret Stream, 24″ × 32″, by Mary Diamond, 2008.

just sign here

"Solstice Stars at the Cabin"
Made for Zoey and Nick
by
Lura Schwarz Smith, Betty Davis,
Betty Magan, Betty Robinson,
Donna Butts and Sharon Hebrard
Quilted by: Kelly Gallagher-Abbott
Copyright 2007
by Lura Schwarz Smith
P.O. Box 649
Coarsegold, CA 93614

This is the label for our daughter's wedding quilt, a group project made with the help of special friends. The photo of our daughter and son-in-law receiving the quilt adds another fun memory to the gift.

LABELS AND LAYERS

With all the time and effort that we put into making a quilt, sometimes we skimp on a very important final detail—the label. Digital imagery is a natural way to create a unique label. You can use your images from the quilt and add text by using layers. By using a digital image from your quilt, your label will be an important addition to your quilt.

IT'S EASY TO ADD TEXT

The secret to placing text in your picture and getting it where you want it is to have the rulers on the top and side of your image window turned on. For example, let's say you want to place text so it is centered in your picture. As you move your cursor in the picture, you will see its exact location in the *ruler* guide along the edges of the picture window. To view rulers in the Full Edit window, select *View > Rulers*. (See pages 27–28 for the details of adding text.)

Saving your file as a Master with layers will allow you to change the line of text. Just before you create your final Target file, flatten the layers (page 29). But keep in mind—once you flatten the layers, the text will be part of the image and cannot easily be changed.

To create a faded out or ghosted area in your picture where you can place text, use the Eraser tool on the background layer. This is one of those cases where less is more: In the *Eraser* menu above the main window, use the slider to reduce your opacity to 25%; then make short sweeps with your brush (see caption on bottom of page 72 for using the Eraser tool). If you overdo the erasing, short brushstrokes make it easier to back up in Undo History and start again.

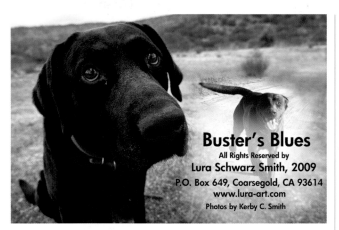

For the best readability, use a heavy or bold type font in a large size when placing text over a grayed-out background. Here is the label for *Buster's Blues* (page 70).

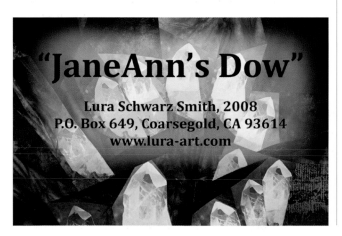

"Honeymoon 1944"
By Lura Schwarz Smith, 2008
P.O. Box 649, Coarsegold, CA 93614 - www.lura-art.com

This is the label from Lura's quilt *Honeymoon 1944* (page 53). The picture of her mother receiving the quilt added another memory to it. There wasn't an appropriate spot to add text in the image; instead, the canvas was increased along the bottom edge to make room for the text.

"JaneAnn's Dow"
Lura Schwarz Smith, 2008
P.O. Box 649, Coarsegold, CA 93614
www.lura-art.com

To create the label for *JaneAnn's Dow* (page 60), text was layered over a ghosted central area in the picture. The faded part of the image for placing text was created using the Eraser tool at 30% opacity.

Another idea for labels is to scan your own artwork, or use copyright-free images, for a different look. For our daughter's Winter Solstice wedding, digitally printed images stitched to wired ribbons made personalized wedding favor ornaments for the guests. Each of these had a hand-drawn look, but to do more than 100 of them by hand would not have been possible. Digital printing made the project fun. The possibilities of using digital imagery are as wide as your imagination.

After taking a photograph for reference and then tracing it (page 78) Lura made a pencil drawing of our daughter's and son-in-law's hands. Of course, the photo could be used instead, but drawing is so much fun.

A scan of the drawing, plus text, made commemorative wedding favor ornaments.

RESOURCES

Many materials and supplies used in this book can be found at your local quilting, art, craft, or office supply stores. Here are some contacts to help you find what you need.

Color Textiles Inc.

Color Plus printable treated fabric sheets and rolls
Phone: 702-838-5868
www.colorplusfabrics.com

Dharma Trading Co.

Textile markers, paints, inks, pastels
Phone: 800-542-5227
www.dharmatrading.com

Dick Blick Art Materials

Colored pencils, markers, paint sticks, textile paints, and pastels
Phone: 800-723-2787
Fax: 800-621-8293
www.dickblick.com

The Electric Quilt Company

EQ Printables printable fabric sheets
Phone: 800-356-4219
www.electricquilt.com

Jacquard Products

Inkjet printing sheets, including ExtravOrganza
www.jacquardproducts.com

Jukebox Quilts

Jukebox has produced two instructional DVDs of Lura's techniques: Faces in Fabric *for inking and shading and* From Snapshots to Art Quilts *for design elements. Jukebox is also a source for Tsukineko Inks, Fantastix, Fabrico Markers, and ink stands.*

Phone: 970-224-9975
Fax: 970-224-4260
www.jukeboxquilts.com

Milliken & Company

Printable treated fabric sheets
www.printedtreasures.com

Tsukineko, Inc.

Inks, Fantastix, Fabrico Markers, and ink stands
Phone: 425-883-7733
Fax: 425-883-7418
www.tsukineko.com

Suggested Reading

DESIGN

Aimone, Steven. *Design! A Lively Guide to Design Basics for Artists & Craftspeople.* Lark Books, 2007

Masopust, Katie Pasquini. *Design Explorations for the Creative Quilter.* C&T Publishing, 2008.

Masopust, Katie Pasquini, and Brett Barker. *Color and Composition for the Creative Quilter.* C&T Publishing, 2005.

Torrence, Lorraine, and Jean B. Mills. *Fearless Design for Every Quilter.* C&T Publishing, 2009.

INKJET PRINTING ON FABRIC

Halligan, Krista Camacho. *Photo-Fabric Play.* C&T Publishing, 2008.

Hewlett Packard Company, edited by Cyndy Lyle Rymer. *Photo Fun.* C&T Publishing, 2004.

Hewlett Packard Company, Cyndy Lyle Rymer, and Lynn Koolish. *More Photo Fun.* C&T Publishing, 2004.

Koolish, Lynn. *Lynn Koolish Teaches You Printing on Fabric* (DVD). C&T Publishing, 2008.

Rymer, Cyndy, with Lynn Koolish. *Innovative Fabric Imagery.* C&T Publishing, 2007.

Wheeler, Beth, and Lori Marquette. *Altered Photo Artistry.* C&T Publishing, 2007.

PHOTOSHOP ELEMENTS

Kelby, Scott. *Adobe Photoshop . . . for Digital Photographers* (series). New Riders Press.

Brundage, Barbara. *Photoshop Elements: The Missing Manual* (series). Pogue Press.

QUILTMAKING

Anderson, Alex. *Start Quilting with Alex Anderson.* C&T Publishing, 2001.

Goldsmith, Becky, and Linda Jenkins. *Piecing the Piece O' Cake Way.* C&T Publishing, 2007.

Hargrave, Harriet, Sharyn Craig, Alex Anderson, and Liz Aneloski. *All-in-One Quilter's Reference Tool.* C&T Publishing, 2004.

Wasilowski, Laura. *Fusing Fun.* C&T Publishing, 2005

Wells, Jean. *Intuitive Color & Design.* C&T Publishing, 2009.

about the authors

PHOTO BY CAROLYN AND MIKE INGLIS

Lura Schwarz Smith has a Bachelor of Arts degree in art from San Francisco State University. She has been producing art quilts for more than 30 years. Lura started showing her quilts in galleries in the 1970s and 1980s, and over the years she has shown quilts and received awards at regional, national, and international quilt shows. One of her quilts was included in the 100 Best American Quilts of the 20th Century. In addition to returning to her gallery roots, Lura and her husband, Kerby, have enjoyed teaming up to teach digital quilt classes and to produce art quilts using digital imagery. Of course, their best collaborative work resulted in their two children, Zoey and Gary.

Kerby C. Smith spent thirty-five years in journalism working as a free-lance journalist and photojournalist for leading newspapers and magazines in America. He has covered everything from anti-war riots to the first landing of the Space Shuttle. While assignments for *National Geographic Magazine* took him around the world, he is most at home in America's West. He has written, edited, and produced magazines, books, and television documentaries. His past nine years in marketing have honed the communications skills he uses to create advertising campaigns that sell products. He has been married to art quilter Lura Schwarz Smith for more than 31 wonderful years.

Visit Lura and Kerby at their website, www.thedigitalquilt.com, where you will find updates to the technical information in this book, descriptions of classes we teach, and our blog. For information on Lura's work and class schedule, visit www.lura-art.com.

Great Titles *from* C&T PUBLISHING

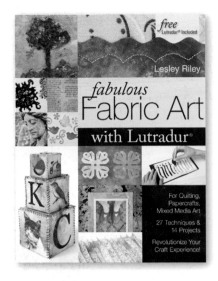

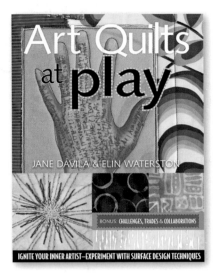

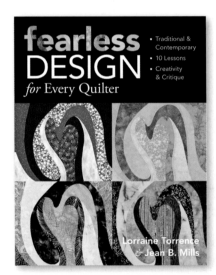

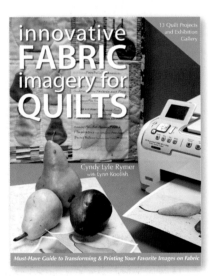

Available at your local retailer or **www.ctpub.com** *or* **800.284.1114**

For a list of other fine books from C&T Publishing, ask for a free catalog:

C&T PUBLISHING, INC.
P.O. Box 1456
Lafayette, CA 94549
(800) 284-1114

Email: ctinfo@ctpub.com
Website: www.ctpub.com

C&T Publishing's professional photography services are now available to the public. Visit us at www.ctmediaservices.com.

Tips and Techniques can be found at www.ctpub.com > Consumer Resources > Quiltmaking Basics: Tips & Techniques for Quiltmaking & More

For quilting supplies:

COTTON PATCH
1025 Brown Ave.
Lafayette, CA 94549
Store: (925) 284-1177
Mail order: (925) 283-7883

Email: CottonPa@aol.com
Website: www.quiltusa.com

Note: Fabrics used in the quilts shown may not be currently available, as fabric manufacturers keep most fabrics in print for only a short time.